NANCY

NANCY

by Nancy Reagan
with Bill Libby

WILLIAM MORROW AND COMPANY, INC.
New York   *1980*

Portions of this book previously appeared in *Good Housekeeping*.

Library of Congress Cataloging in Publication Data

Reagan, Nancy, 1923–
    Nancy.

    1. Reagan, Nancy, 1923– 2. Reagan, Ronald.
3. Actors—United States—Biography. 4. California
—Governors—Wives—Biography. I. Libby, Bill,
joint author. II. Title.
CT275.R323A36   979.4′05′0924 [B]   79-26509
ISBN 0-688-03533-7

Printed in the United States of America

First Edition

1 2 3 4 5 6 7 8 9 10

Book Design by Michael Mauceri

To Ronnie, who was always there when I needed help, who always had a word of encouragement, and who is so much a part of my story.

Acknowledgments

Many people have helped make this book possible. I can't hope to include them all on this page, but among them are: Mike Deaver, who has helped us in so many ways during the years of politics and public life; Bill Adler, who first suggested the book and who introduced me to the publisher; Pete Hanna-ford and Nancy Reynolds for their encouragement and suggestions; Bill Libby, who converted my taped reminiscences to written form; Jackie Sommers, who transcribed our tapes; Gwen Pruter, Elaine Crispen, Leslie Ohland, Barbara Perillo, Sandy Stern, Faye Hill, Dodie Livingston, and Dottie Dellinger for their unfailing good cheer during the hours they typed and proof-read the manuscript.

NANCY DAVIS REAGAN

Pacific Palisades
July 1979

9

Introduction

This is Nancy Reagan's book, not Ronald Reagan's, this writer's, or anyone else's. It is her personal feeling about her life in particular and life in general, and all this writer did was to organize the words she put on tape and put them on paper.

So that in your mind you will be able to hear her as she spoke the words you will read in this book and see her as she sat in or moved about the rooms of the Reagan home in Pacific Palisades, California, I should describe her and her setting.

She is a small, lovely woman with fine features who seems to be at least ten years younger than her actual age. She has hazel eyes that glow with light when she is happy about something and give off sparks when she is unhappy. She is relaxed and laughs easily. She is sentimental and tears come fast to her eyes. But when those sparks fly, watch out. She is strong and strong-willed. She makes you want to be her friend, but all the while you feel she would be tough in a fight.

Nancy Reagan is outspoken, yet protective of her privacy. She is modest about her own accomplishments, but because she has had such a changing life, has been exposed to so many awesome arenas, and has learned so much from so many varied experiences, she found she had a lot to say. She is highly intelligent and articulate and speaks softly with a warm voice, but she speaks firmly and is careful to say what she wants to say. She is not intimidated by public pressures or the bright, hot glare of the spotlight, and she is herself at all times.

Wherever Nancy goes, she is asked about Hollywood and her husband, and about life in general. In this book she has attempted to answer many of those questions. More than a former actress and wife of an actor and more than the wife of the former governor of California, she is a wife of more than twenty-five years to the only husband she has ever had, a man she clearly loves and admires, and a mother to their children, now adults.

Ronald Reagan is an affable man, charming and easy with people, warm and witty, down-to-earth and unpretentious. You can sit down and talk with him about football or films and forget what he has been and what he may be. He is a great storyteller and a good friend to many. Even his most outspoken political enemies have found it hard to dislike him, and the reporters who have traveled the campaign trail with him admit it is impossible not to like him.

He is a devoted husband and father, a new and devoted grand-father. Like any other grandfather, when he holds the grandson his son Michael presented him in 1978, his still-handsome face lights up. When Ronald and Nancy Reagan meet and part, they embrace and kiss. They touch one another. They care. They are not ashamed to show it, or embarrassed by the presence of others. It is not difficult to tell what is real and unreal. Their feeling for one another is real.

They both seem younger than their years. Ronald keeps a prodigious pace, even out of public office—writing, doing a radio show, giving speeches. He flies here and there, in and out of the country. He is seldom home. She keeps pulling him homeward, seeking prized days of privacy with him, protecting him from his desire to do even more than he does. She travels with him at times, especially in campaign years. She is a terrific campaigner. But she is alone a great deal, and she has learned to do a lot independently and to make the most of a life in which she is alone and on her own.

Nancy believes in Ronnie and supports him. She says she cannot imagine life without him. She gave up her former life to be his wife and mother to his children. "I am a nester," she says. She is feminine and perhaps old-fashioned in today's world. She believes in women's rights. She has fought for her rights and lives her own life, but she adjusts it to his. She cannot imagine getting anything that would be worth giving up being his wife. She is more forgiving of faults in others than she would be of those in herself. She does not preach her principles, but she does believe in them.

Nancy Reagan stands 5 feet, 4 inches tall, and weighs 109 pounds. She watches her weight, but eats what she wants and does not gain. She loses weight by worrying. "I'm a worrier," she admits. "I don't worry so much about myself, but I worry about Ronnie and the kids and the world. I worry if I don't have anything to worry about," she adds, laughing. She is slender, graceful, and stylish, and wears clothes well. She dresses simply and looks as good in jeans as in a tailored suit. She never looks mussed up. Women of the press who have traveled with her and know how wearing her schedule can be, marvel that they become disheveled and she doesn't.

Home to her is both the house they have owned for almost twenty-five years, high in the hills off Sunset Boulevard above the Pacific Ocean, and the ranch they have maintained in the mountains near Santa Barbara since he left office in Sacramento. The ranch is 600-plus acres of wooded beauty, and the Reagans redid the small 90-year-old adobe house with their own hands. ("If you wanted to see me mussed up you should have been there," she says, smiling. "And with paint in my hair, too.") The ranch is their refuge. They have a foreman, but it is their place; there they ride horses and keep dogs and other animals. She is a lover of animals. She picks strays up off highways at night and takes them home with her. At the ranch there is beauty and time to enjoy it, time to themselves, and peace away from the world.

"We walk the beach, holding hands like kids. I could sit and watch the waves without wanting to leave for hours," she says.

Though close to it, their house in the Pacific Palisades is out of sight of the sea, surrounded by the Santa Monica Mountains. It is up a steep and curving road, set apart from others

13

there. It is a spacious house, though far from a mansion. There is a housekeeper, Anne, who has been with them for years. She cooks and keeps the place neat, but it looks lived in and the parties there are private and small, for friends. Two dogs —a large Belgian Shepherd and a small Cockapoo—protect the place from enemies, bark loudly at any car that comes up the curving driveway, and nuzzle Nancy delightedly at every opportunity. "Barney" Barnett, a former California Highway Patrolman and member of the governor's security detail, has been with them since Sacramento and is more a part of the family than an employee. He is paid, but his is a labor of love.

The furnishings are antique or Oriental. The paintings on the walls are Spanish or traditional. The photos on the grand piano or tables or shelves are of the Reagans posed not only with prominent politicians or world leaders but with friends from the film community, such as James Cagney and John Wayne.

The taping of this book took place in the living room and in the small den overlooking the swimming pool. Both rooms are filled with flowers and books, as are most of the rooms of this house. Both are important to her life. On a lower bookshelf lies a bound book of stills from her films, but other than the photos of friends there is little here to remind anyone of their screen careers. Although Ronnie has been given countless awards, there are few plaques on the walls. Nothing is there for show.

The phone rings constantly. Not only for him but for her. She is involved in several charities, most notably the one she helped create for the elderly—the Foster Grandparent Program —which has spread across the country. She does not waste time or passion in pursuit of frivolous pleasures, although she is known among her friends for her infectious laugh.

So that you do not have to seek them out, here are some of the facts and dates of her story:

She was born Anne Frances Robbins on July 6, 1923. Her mother is the former actress Edith Luckett of Petersburg, Virginia. Nancy's father was Kenneth Robbins, but he separated from her mother and they divorced soon afterward.

When she was two, Nancy went to live in Bethesda, Maryland, with her mother's sister and brother-in-law, Virginia and Audley Galbraith, and their daughter Charlotte. Nancy's mother married Loyal Davis on May 20, 1929, and Nancy went to live with them on Chicago's North Lakeshore.

Loyal Davis was a pioneer neurosurgeon, who became Chairman of the Department of Surgery at Northwestern University Medical School and Chief of Surgery at Passavant Memorial Hospital in Chicago. He has been made an Honorary Fellow of the Royal Colleges of Surgeons of England and Edinburgh. She considers him her father. He and her mother now live in Phoenix, Arizona.

Nancy graduated from Smith College in Northampton, Massachusetts, and stayed with her mother in Chicago until her father returned from overseas assignments during World War II. She became an actress, first appearing in plays touring the country, then on Broadway. After doing a little television, she was called to Hollywood and went to work in the film community, where she and her mother had so many friends.

She made eleven movies between 1949 and 1956, probably the most memorable being a Dore Schary project, *The Next Voice You Hear*. She met Ronnie in 1951 and married him a year later, on March 4, 1952. They have a daughter, Patricia Ann, and a son, Ronald Prescott, as well as two children by his previous marriage, Maureen and Michael.

Ronald Wilson Reagan was born on February 6, 1911, in Tampico, Illinois. He was an athlete at Eureka College, Illinois, and became a sports announcer in Iowa. He was broadcasting Chicago Cubs' games at spring training on Catalina Island, California, when he landed a screen contract with Warner Brothers. He made fifty-four films between 1937 and 1964, portraying most memorably Notre Dame's great George Gipp in *Knute Rockne—All American*, and an amputee in *Kings Row*. He went into television and hosted not only *Death Valley Days* but *General Electric Theater*, and also served as a goodwill ambassador across the country for GE.

He was active in film-industry politics and served six years as president of the Screen Actors Guild. Originally a Democrat, eventually he became a Republican, and grew increasingly active in national and state politics. He challenged the incumbent California governor Edmund "Pat" Brown, became governor himself in 1966, and was reelected in 1970. He campaigned for

15

the presidency in 1976 and won the majority of his primary tests against President Ford, but lost the battle to the incumbent for the Republican nomination at the GOP convention.

Nancy Reagan is not a person who worries about dates and details. She is most concerned about the events and experiences, the emotions and insights of an unusual, inspirational life, and this she provides in the pages that follow.

BILL LIBBY

1979

NANCY

Chapter 1

I don't suppose we ever expect what happens to us in our lives, but I never thought I would be the wife of the governor of California, and I certainly never expected my husband would be persuaded to enter the presidential arena. I expected to marry, have children, and lead an "ordinary" life, except for me being a wife and mother is not ordinary—it is an extraordinary and fulfilling way of life.

My mother often told me, "Don't ever say you'll *never* do something because that may be exactly what you end up doing." She was an actress, and at one time in my life I hoped to be an actress, but I did not wish to be one forever. Mother gave up acting when she married, and I expected to do the same.

Well, I did become an actress. I acted on Broadway and in Hollywood, but one thing I didn't expect was that I would marry an actor. I seldom dated actors, and if I had not met Ronald Reagan, it is a pretty good bet that I would not have married one. Unlike most performers I had met, he had interests beyond the stage and screen. From the moment we met, I think I was aware that acting was not enough for him, that he might turn to other things in life, and I was prepared to go wherever he went and make a home for us wherever we landed. Although he was involved in film politics, I didn't expect him to get involved in real politics, something in which I had never had any interest.

I have said many times that my life really began when I married my husband, and I think to a great extent it did. Of course, I had a life before he came along, but it seems to have been primarily preparation for the real one that would follow.

His course in life carried me into the spotlight far more than my career ever did. For all of the ups and downs of a political career, it certainly has been interesting and has given me the chance to contribute a little, to pay my way for the good things life has brought me.

Ronald Reagan has made my life more eventful and exciting than I could have ever dreamed it would be, yet it was somewhat eventful and exciting before I met him.

Life began for me in July 1923 in New York City. When I was a young actress, I once refused to give the year of my birth to a magazine writer. All young actresses are twenty-two. When the story was published the writer had guessed at my age and made me five years older than I was. I immediately wrote the magazine asking them to give me back my five years because I had plans for them. They printed my letter but I learned a good lesson. When you're asked a question, it's better to give an answer, or someone will give one for you and it may not be correct or what you want!

I was born in a hospital in Manhattan. I don't remember the name of the hospital, but I know it has long since burned down. I was due on the fourth of July, but my mother, as she tells it, was a baseball fan who was determined to see a doubleheader on that day. Knowing her, I believe it.

When she arrived at the hospital two days later, she was told there was no room and she would have to go elsewhere. My mother is a strong-willed woman. She lay down in the middle of the reception room floor and said, "Well, I guess I'll have my baby right here." Everyone bustled around and miraculously discovered they had had a room all the time.

It was a hot day, and the last thing she remembered in the delivery room was the doctor talking about how hot it was and how he wanted to get it over with so he could get out on the golf course. It turned out to be a difficult forceps delivery, and when I was brought to her, my right eye was closed. The doctor told her I might be blind in that eye. She told him that she had heard what he had said in the delivery room and that if my eye didn't open she would kill him. Fortunately for him, after two weeks my eye opened. To tell you the truth, I'm not sure she wouldn't have carried out her threat. The only reminder I have of this is a scar on the right side of my face which has gradually faded over the years.

I was born Anne Frances Robbins. However, as long as I can remember, I have been called by the diminutive "Nancy." My mother was born Edith Luckett, and she was married to Kenneth Robbins. He had worked for his father in the woolen mills in his hometown of Pittsfield, Massachusetts, but was selling cars in New Jersey when I was born. He and my mother separated immediately after I arrived, and Mother resumed her career as a stage actress that she had given up when she had married.

I was told later that my father wasn't at the hospital when I was born, which must have hurt Mother as much as it did me when I heard about it. I have no idea how old I was before he saw me for the first time, but I visited him only a few times over the years before he died in the 1960's. He was my father, but I somehow never could think of him that way because there had never been any relationship of any kind.

My mother was one of nine children born to Sarah Frances Whitlock and Charles Edward Luckett of Petersburg, Virginia. My grandfather worked for the Adams Express Company, which later became the Railway Express. In time, he was transferred to Washington, D.C., but Sarah was a real rebel who returned to Virginia to have each of her children because she wasn't going to give birth to any "damn Yankees."

Times were tough for the Lucketts with their large family. Few of the children attended school for very long. They had to go to work. Mother's brother Joe had gone into the theater business, which is how she got started as an actress.

Uncle Joe was managing a theater in Washington which billed stock companies and featured John Mason, John Drew, and many other stars of the day. A child in one of the shows became ill, and Uncle Joe substituted his baby sister. Mother had to die in the play and did it so convincingly she had the audience in tears. At the curtain call, she raised herself up and waved to let the people know she was really all right. I don't think the management was thrilled with this, but the audience loved it. As the story goes, she received an ovation and it was music to her ears. She was hooked on show business and was acting full time at the age of fifteen.

One of her first jobs was with Chauncey Alcott. His sister, who accompanied him on the piano while he sang "My Wild Irish Rose," became ill and Mother applied for the job. Mr. Alcott asked if she played the piano, and although she did not, she told him she did, and so he hired her. She went out, bought a toy piano, and stayed up all night practicing. The next night she appeared with Mr. Alcott, playing "My Wild Irish Rose" on the piano, and no one ever suspected. Right from the first, Mother was a trouper, and I've often said they broke the mold after they made her.

Mother played with the greats of her day, including David Belasco, George M. Cohan, and Alla Nazimova. She appeared with many stage performers who later became prominent in films, such as Walter Huston, Louis Calhern, Zasu Pitts, and Spencer Tracy. In her last Broadway appearance in 1928, she played with Walter Huston and Kay Francis in *Elmer the Great*. I have all of her scrap books, and last Christmas I showed them to our children. She was—and is—beautiful, inside and out, and I was always proud of her.

I was about two years old when Mother took me to live with my aunt and uncle Virginia and Audley Galbraith and their daughter, my cousin Charlotte, in Bethesda, Maryland. Mother wanted me to have as normal an upbringing as possible. Traveling around in a stage trunk certainly wouldn't provide that. It was a terrible wrench for both of us. Whenever Mother landed in New York for any length of time, my aunt would take me there by train to live with her. Although I was very young when I made these visits, they were so important to me that I still have some vivid impressions.

When Mother was in New York, she used to live in residential hotels or in brownstone front apartments. To this day, I can't pass this type of building without getting a terrible sinking feeling in my stomach. It triggers the memory of how much I missed

Mother when I was apart from her, how I looked forward to and loved my visits with her, how few visits there were, and how I always had to leave. Years later after Ronnie and I were married, we were east on a trip, and I found myself in one of those hotels. I became so depressed that I finally had to explain to Ronnie why, and he said, "That's it, we'll move to another hotel," which we did. I felt foolish but I must admit I felt better, too. I guess that's why it is so difficult for me to understand some of today's children who express such hostility toward their parents and who apparently cannot wait to leave them. If they leave out the parent-child relationship in their lives, they are leaving out a lot. They don't know what they are missing and, sadly, may not find out until it's too late.

The visits with Mother were wonderful. I loved to dress up in her stage clothes, put on her makeup, and pretend I was playing her parts. I saw her shows over and over again and never tired of them. Usually, I sat in the audience, but sometimes I watched from the wings. I don't remember the names of the plays, but I do remember the faces of the actors and actresses and the stagehands. The stagehands were especially nice to me. One built me a large doll's house as a present, which I treasured. There's a particular "smell" to backstage that's hard to describe, but it's rather musty and to me always seemed glamorous and special. I can bring it back to mind today.

When I went into acting later, my mother warned me that I had seen only the glamorous side of the profession—when she had a role in a successful play on Broadway. I had not seen the other side of the business—when she was in less successful plays or flops, when she failed to get parts, or when she was out of work. However, I never thought of what she did as being "glamorous." This was just what she did.

Most of the time it seemed like something fun to do, but I remember one play where her part called for being treated unkindly by the other characters, and it upset me terribly. I watched from a box out front, and when I went backstage after the show, I was crying and wouldn't talk to anyone because I thought they had been mean to my mother. I suppose the others thought it was funny, but they did try to console me. My mother had to take me aside to tell me, "Nancy, you can't take this sort

23

of thing seriously. It's not real. It's make-believe. It's a play and I'm playing a part. The other actors don't really dislike me."

I lived with the Galbraiths for about five years, until I was almost seven. They treated me wonderfully well, as if I were their own daughter, and I loved them, but I was lonesome for my mother. When I was four or five years old, I had double pneumonia and was seriously ill for a while. My aunt and uncle took care of me as well as anyone could, but I wanted my mother with me and she was somewhere out on the road away from me. No matter how kind someone is to you, it is just not the same as when it is your mother. I can remember crying at this time and saying, "If I had a child and she got sick, I'd be with her." Now that I have children myself, I realize how much it must have hurt my mother, especially since she had no choice. She had to work.

However, I had a happy time with Aunt Virginia and Uncle Audley and Charlotte in Bethesda, and have wonderful memories of it. We lived in a tiny, tiny house, which I can describe today down to the last detail. But they made room for me and made me happy.

The big treat of the week for Charlotte and me came on Saturday night, when Uncle Audley would take us to the basement and give us each a large piece of milk chocolate. I have no idea where he got it, but he had a new one each week, and how we looked forward to it. When you don't have a lot, small treats loom large. Candy has never tasted as good before or since.

Charlotte was three or four years older than I and could have resented the place I took in her family, but she didn't, and we were more like sisters than cousins. Despite the difference in our ages, we played together a great deal. We used to play "Kick the Can" and "Statues" in the empty lot next door after dinner, and I would take dolls and toy dishes out in front of the house and give pretend parties.

Bethesda was a typical small town, and as in most small towns in those days, the Fourth of July celebration was the big event. There were speeches, picnics, fireworks, and a parade. One Fourth of July, Charlotte decorated her bicycle and I decorated our wire-haired dog, Ginger, and we joined the parade.

Those were good old times in the good old days, a peaceful time in a peaceful place, when we ate ice cream in the summer and slid down a snowy hill in the winter. I remember Bethesda with affection.

My aunt and uncle are gone now. Charlotte lives in Atlanta with her husband, Jim Ramage, an insurance man, but we keep in touch. They have children, including a daughter named Nancy in my honor, which means a lot to me.

As I noted earlier, I visited with my father a few times when I was young. He had remarried, and his wife was a very nice woman who tried to make me welcome on my visits. They once took me on a trip to Niagara Falls. My father tried to please me, but too many years had gone by and we were really strangers to each other. As I look back, I am sure he was unhappy about it. Since Kenneth Robbins was such a small part of my life, it is impossible for me to think of him as my father.

But I remember well my last visit to their apartment in New Jersey when things went badly. He said something about Mother I didn't like and it made me angry. I said I was going to call my mother and go home. He got upset and locked me in the bathroom. I was terrified, and it seemed suddenly as if I were with strangers. Recalling the incident brings back a flood of memories I would rather forget. To this day, I dislike locked doors and feel trapped behind them.

His wife felt terrible and later wrote to my mother to apologize, but there were no more visits.

My father's mother, Anne, a handsome, gray-haired woman, did not want to lose contact with her only grandchild. I remember she always used a violet toilet water whose aroma I can still smell. She came to see me in California just before Ronnie and I were married. The three of us were having dinner at Chasen's when she suffered a stroke. We rushed her to the hospital, and although she recovered, she died not too long afterward.

My father died soon after his wife had passed away. Ronnie was governor at the time and we were living in Sacramento. Before he died, Eleanor Harris wrote a piece about me for *Look* magazine. She knew my family in Chicago, so, of course, she knew my background. She touched on it in the story, but it was never picked up by the press, for which I was grateful. My father was still alive, and I didn't want to say something that might hurt him.

But I did consider Loyal Davis to be my father. He came into my life, and became a big part of it, one day in the early spring of 1929.

Mother had come to see me in Bethesda. She took me out on the screened porch of that little house and told me she had met and fallen in love with a doctor, Loyal Davis. She wanted to marry him, but she would not do so if I didn't want her to. If I agreed, however, she would give up the stage and we would live together in Chicago.

Well, I was not yet seven years old and did not have a very sophisticated view of what she was telling me. But, as it seemed to mean living with my mother, I was all for it. I shiver sometimes when I think that I might have said no; it would have been the mistake of my life. On second thought, I am sure Mother would have talked me out of that decision. She seemed very happy, as she had every right to be, for he was a fine man, although I didn't know it at the time.

Years later I came across the journal of Mother's trip when she met the "doctor she wanted to marry." It had been a shipboard romance. She was traveling with friends, and he was going to a medical convention in England. Each day she would describe her meeting with him and what they had done. But at the bottom of each page, she would write, "How I miss my baby." I cried when I first read it, and still get a lump in my throat at the thought.

Mother had to finish her tour with *Elmer the Great* in Chicago. Later, Aunt Virginia took me on the train to meet her there. Although I was very happy to be going to live with my mother, I could not help feeling a little unhappy about leaving the Galbraiths, who had been wonderful to me. I was leaving the town that was the only home I had known, a town where I had friends, and going to a new home in a big city where I knew no one. Six years old and scared, but I was going to be with Mother at last.

There was an early-season heat wave at that time, and it was unbearably hot on the train. We opened one of the windows, but soot and dirt blew in, soiling our dressy clothes. So we closed the window and suffered the heat. But finally we arrived and were met at the station by my mother and the man who was to be my father.

I was a flower girl at their wedding in May 1929 at the Fourth Presbyterian Church in Chicago.

So I began a new period in my life—one which I was to discover would be very happy, and one in which I grew up and began to develop many of the principles in which I believe today.

I had a few rough times in the beginning. I was overjoyed to be living with Mother, but I was jealous of having to share her with Dr. Davis, a man I really did not know. Fortunately, he was kind and sensitive enough to recognize this and handled the situation delicately and wisely. He didn't rush in and declare I was his, like it or not. He told me that he and my mother loved one another, that he would be good to her. He didn't think it would be right to adopt me automatically because my real father was still alive, but if I ever wanted him to, nothing would make him happier. He also said that he hoped he and I would come to love one another, too. He would try to do his best by me and hoped we would become a family. He would give it time.

It did not take too much time. He was—and is—a man of more strength and integrity than any I have known other than Ronnie, and as I grew up I came to understand this and to love and respect him. He added a dimension to my life I am sure I would not have had without him.

Some people you meet in your life make you stretch to reach your fullest capabilities. I found my new father to be one of these people, which is why he made such a good teacher when he was Professor of Surgery at Northwestern University. He always demanded the best of you and made you want to give the best you had. He was strict but fair with me, as he was with his students. They came to respect him as I came to respect him. When he took privileges away from me as punishment for some misdeed, I understood I deserved the discipline. He was, I feel, the way a father should be.

Loyal Davis grew up in Galesburg, Illinois, the son of a railroad engineer. For a while he thought that is what he also wanted to be. His father took him on rides in the engineer's cab to let him see what the job was really like, and, I am sure, to encourage him to consider other careers. Then, a doctor befriended him, and he decided to pursue medicine.

His family had little money, and he worked his way through college and medical school, succeeding through hard work. He studied at Knox College and Northwestern University. Once, early in his term at the university, he became discouraged and was on the verge of quitting. He went down to the railway depot, knowing his father was taking his train out of Galesburg. It was a cold winter night with snow falling heavily. His father never said a word about his son's decision to give up medical school. He put my father on the fireman's seat and just "accidentally" broke the cab window on that side with a wrench. They rode to Galesburg with the snow and bitter cold blowing in through the broken window. When they arrived, his father did not let him off at the station, but took the engine out into the yards on a siding, which meant walking about a mile back through the near blizzard. That was the last time my father thought about giving up medicine.

He served his residency at Cook County Hospital in Chicago, and studied with such pioneers of surgery as Walter Dandy in Baltimore, Charles Frazier in Philadelphia, Charles Elsberg in New York, and Harvey Cushing in Boston.

Cushing is considered "the father of neurosurgery" in this country, and my father dedicated himself to this specialty. He served as an associate in surgery at Peter Bent Brigham Hospital in Boston in the 1920's and returned to Chicago to become the first full-time practitioner of brain surgery in that great city. He later served as chief of surgery at Passavant Northwestern University Memorial Hospital in Chicago for about thirty years, and as chairman of the Department of Surgery at Northwestern for many years.

He served his country in both world wars. During World War II, he developed a helmet to protect pilots from shrapnel wounds that was the prototype of the present aviation helmet. He perfected the treatment of high-altitude frost-bite injuries. He was a member of a surgical mission to Moscow in 1944 and was awarded the Legion of Merit medal in 1945.

A man of the highest principles, he took on the medical establishment in many memorable battles. He spoke out against the unfortunate practice of fee-splitting, in which doctors refer patients to specialists or surgeons who kick back a portion of their payment. And he fought the practice of unnecessary surgery, in which doctors cut their patients before exhausting other alternatives. He was and is a very independent, outspoken man and always expresses his opinion. This did not always make him the most popular man around, but you always knew where you stood with him.

A founder of the American Board of Surgery and American Board of Neurological Surgery, he has been chairman of the board and president of the American College of Surgeons, editor of *Christopher's Textbook of Surgery*, and editor of the surgical journal, *Surgery, Gynecology and Obstetrics*—a job he performs today. He was conferred honorary fellowships in the Royal Colleges of Surgeons in England and Edinburgh.

My parents' marriage is an ideal one, and each has given to the other what was needed. My father always said my mother made it possible for him to have a life beyond his professional commitments, a social life with family and friends he had not enjoyed before. He retained the desire and drive to do well in his profession, but developed the ability to relax with family and friends. He was not socially outgoing or a partygoer, but Mother was a gregarious woman and soon brought him out of his shell. She probably helped enhance his professional standing by improving his social contacts because she naturally attracted people to her.

If I can be one-fourth the woman my mother is, I would be happy. She is a beautiful and talented woman, strong but sensitive. She has dealt with hard times but maintained her sense of humor throughout—a trait that stands a person in good stead, as I was to discover later. She is also one of the best storytellers around, which all of her friends will attest to. Better known by her nicknames of "Lucky" or "DeeDee" than by any formal names, it sometimes seems that she knows everyone in the world —every taxi driver, every traffic cop—every everyone.

I remember one time after she married Dr. Davis, she was in a beauty shop when a young girl came in saying she was going to marry one of the sailors at the Navy Yard and did not know where they could have the wedding. They were married at our apartment.

Another time, Ronnie and I arrived in Chicago by train when there was a porters' strike and no one was available to pick up our luggage. Mother came to meet us with a Red Cap porter on each arm, saying to one of them, "Well, now, how is Johnny, are his tonsils all right now? Because if they're not you have him come right to Dr. Davis and he'll take care of you. And how is Alice and is she feeling all right now? And, oh, here's my daughter and son-in-law, and they have a few little bags to be picked up . . ."

When she became Edie Davis, Mother became the ideal doctor's wife. He was a prominent doctor, and she hosted his social affairs. She even organized and developed the gift shop at Passavant Hospital, which thrived under her fine hand. My father and I both learned from her not to take ourselves too seriously.

Loyal Davis made me a member of a family, and for that I'll be forever grateful to him. He had been married once before and had a son, Richard, who lived with his mother until she died in the late 1930's, when he came to live with us. This made our family complete. He is a couple of years younger than I, a very bright man who followed in his father's footsteps and became a neurosurgeon after studying at Princeton. He is married, has two children of his own, and is presently practicing in Philadelphia. I wish we lived nearer so we could see each other more often, but I feel very close to him.

Since my mother's parents passed on early, I never knew them, so my father's parents were especially important to me. His parents became my grandparents, and wé visited them often in Galesburg and Chicago. They treated me as if I were their real grandchild, and I felt as if I were. They were good, hard-working people, proud of their son, happy with the second marriage he had made, happy with Mother and me. I adored my grandfather and vividly recall the last time I saw him. He was dying of cancer and I went to visit him in Galesburg. We both knew it would be our last time together, although those words were never spoken. We said our good-byes, and as I was leaving, I turned to look back before getting in the car. He was standing at the window and managed a weak wave. I waved back, threw him a kiss, and hurried into the car so he would not see the tears streaming down my face.

Loyal Davis became my legal father when I was fourteen, but emotionally he became my father much earlier than that. It was not long after I started to live with my mother and him that I wanted to be his daughter in every way. He always said it would have to be my choice. There was a law at the time which stipulated that a child had such a choice at the age of fourteen, and when I reached that age, I made my choice. Passing through New York on a vacation, I took the necessary papers for my real father to sign. He signed them, although I'm sure it hurt him to do so. I know it hurt his mother, but it was what I wanted. Loyal Davis became my legal father and I became, officially, Nancy Davis—a far cry from Anne Frances Robbins.

I often accompanied my father to Joliet and other towns around Chicago where he had patients. A neurosurgeon is not as apt to receive emergency calls as some other doctors, but there was always someone who had dived into a lake, despite the posted "No Diving" signs, hitting his head on the rocks in the shallows and damaging his brain and spinal cord. I often went along on these calls to keep my father company, and as a result we became close.

I wanted to see him in action, and I considered it a great privilege when he permitted me to watch some of his operations after I passed into my teens. Usually I watched from a glassed-in balcony, but on one occasion he allowed me to stand beside him in the operating room. He was operating on an elderly man who had developed a nerve disorder which caused a facial twitch and considerable pain. The nerve had to be cut, which would immobilize one side of his face but end the pain. I remember my father saying, "You will hear a noise when the nerve is severed, but there will be no pain." We heard the noise, but the man was sedated. The very next day, I saw the patient sitting up in his hospital bed, seemingly well again.

Like others in his profession, my father seemed to perform miracles, and I was deeply proud of him. I've never watched any other kind of operation and I'm not sure I could, but brain surgery is much cleaner and neater than many others. It's a difficult and delicate operation that requires great training, knowledge, patience, and skill—qualities my father had in abundance.

I had the ability to follow my mother into acting, but could never have followed my father into medicine. Science was never a strong subject for me in school. During the war, however, I did volunteer as a nurse's aide. I had returned to Chicago to be with my mother while my father was away at war. The hospitals were all terribly shorthanded and needed all the help they could get. After completing a training course, I was assigned to Cook County Hospital as a nurse's aide. When I received my assignment, my heart sank. I was assigned to the men's ward—forty men and one nurse. At least they could have assigned me to a women's ward, I felt.

It was horribly hot that first day, and there was no air conditioning in the hospital. We were even giving salt pills to the patients. My first task was to give bed baths. My first patient did not respond to being bathed. His skin seemed strangely cold to me—odd when it was so hot, I told the nurse. She told me to continue. Finally, I told a resident that I was sure something was wrong, and would he please come and look. The poor man had died in the middle of my bed bath!

It is not easy to work in a hospital, but you are giving help to people who need it and helping to save lives, even if some are lost. I was only a nurse's aide, but I was needed at a time when many nurses were serving in the armed forces. I did a lot of dirty work, but it was a job that had to be done. Although I didn't do it for long, it was satisfying. I learned a lot about people and I also discovered what a deep inner satisfaction one can get from giving to people. Your own troubles often seem very small in comparison with those of the sick and injured, and the joy in being able to help, if only just a little, is indescribable. I think I learned an important lesson in life from my hospital work, and I am glad I learned it early. I believe that it pointed the way for me to make contributions to others in hospitals later in life.

I grew up in comfortable circumstances in Chicago. We lived in apartments, first on East Delaware Place, then on Lake Shore Drive. The second apartment was right on Lake Michigan, on the near north side, near the Drake Hotel. I could walk to school

32

My maternal grandparents Sarah and Charles Luckett of Petersburg, Virginia, and one of their nine children, my mother, at the age of two.

Loyal Davis growing up in Galesburg, Illinois. He was the son of a railroad engineer, but became a famous neurosurgeon.

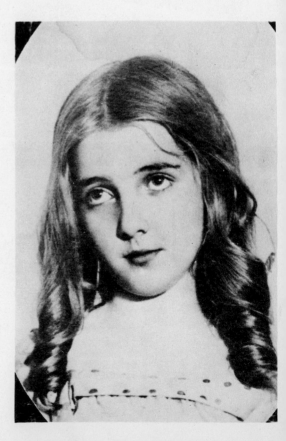

My mother, Edith Luckett, before she became an actress.

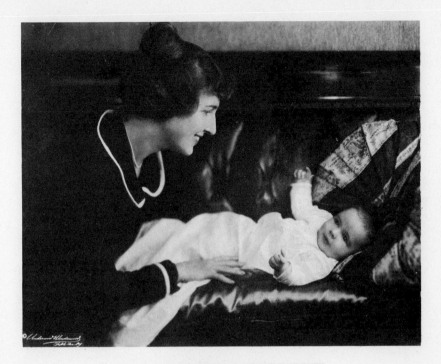

I was born Anne Frances Robbins, but as long as I can remember I have been called "Nancy."

My mother and I were always
very close. It was very difficult
for me when she left.

Meanwhile, Ronnie was growing
up in Illinois.

Our engagement photo in January 1952.

With Ronnie's mother, Nelle, and my parents, we visit Ronnie on a sound stage while he was making a picture.

Here we are with Ardis and Bill Holden, at their house, right after our wedding. Ardis acted under the name Brenda Marshall.

When Patti was christened by Dr. Cleveland Kleihauer, Ardis and Bill
Holden were the godparents and Mrs. Spencer Tracy served as proxy
for godmother Colleen Moore Hargrove.

When Ron was christened by Dr. H. Warren Allen, Bob and Ursula Taylor were his godparents.

—PHOTO BY ROBERT C. FERGUSON

Dr. and Mrs. Loyal Davis, my proud parents after hearing of Patti's birth.

I realize I've been lucky.

My father's portrait that hangs in the lobby of Passavant Memorial Hospital.
—PHOTO: *Chicago Tribune*

Patti decided she would look after her younger brother when we left on a short trip.

Patti and Ron on a happy day at the ranch.

Maureen

Michael, Colleen, and Ronnie's first grandchild, Cameron Michael Reagan.

Ron as a college freshman.

Patti with me at my birthday party.

Ron, Maureen, Michael, and Patti.

along the lake, except in the worst weather, and I loved it, even when it was windy and cold. There were times when it was too windy and cold, when the waves came up too high and hard. At those times I walked along Michigan Avenue around the Drake, which was the windiest spot of all and where ropes were strung from corner to corner so people could cross safely in the slippery, icy weather. There was a tall blond policeman named Tommy on duty there, and I was secretly in love with him. He was nice to all of us. I would tell him I was having trouble, and he'd help me cross while I hung on to his belt.

The apartment had a window box that ran the length of the living room overlooking the water, and I spent hours simply looking at the lake in all of its marvelous moods—smooth and blue and sparkling in the summer sun, wild and grey and driven by the winter winds. I think that is when I first developed my love of the water. I know that if I am upset all I have to do is go down to the ocean. The sight of it, the smell of it, and the sound of it all restore my sense of peace.

Among the highlights of my early years in Chicago were summers spent at Camp Ketchuwa in Michigan. I went there for eight weeks every summer until I was fourteen and loved it. We would swim in the lake before breakfast when it was cool and the air was fresh. The water was so clean and clear we brushed our teeth in the lake water with salt. Our days were spent hiking through the woods, playing tennis, performing plays, doing crafts, and canoeing. Sometimes we would take canoe trips along the lake and be gone for almost a week. We would sleep out under the stars at night.

Sadly, there came a time when I was too old for camp. But I recaptured the feeling again years later when Ronnie and I took our son on a pack trip into the High Sierras. The trip was born one night at the dinner table when our son Ron, then about fifteen, was obviously testing us. He had spent his early childhood going to the ranch with us, seeing his father ride, build fences, and do all of the things that go with ranching. Later, of course, we spent only an occasional weekend in the country, when we were living in Sacramento while Ronnie was governor. Perhaps Ron needed proof that we still liked the active outdoor life or that we still could handle it. At any rate, he dared us to go back-packing with him or, as he put it, "something like that."

That night in our bedroom, Ronnie and I talked it over and decided to propose a pack trip to the High Sierras. The next evening we invited Ron to join us on a four-day horseback trip into the mountains, and of course he accepted enthusiastically. Incidentally, it was a first for all of us as well as for him. Ronnie made all of the plans and arrangements—no tents, just sleeping bags under the stars, horses to ride, and mules to pack the supplies. It was a once-in-a-lifetime experience.

There is really no way to describe such a trip and make it understandable: the long hours in the saddle through unbelievably beautiful scenery; making the camp in late afternoon; food that tasted better than anything you have ever eaten; an evening around the campfire; and finally snuggling down in sleeping bags on the ground.

We caught trout for breakfast and then got back in the saddle to ride even deeper into those magnificent mountains. Each of us carried a Sierra cup, a tin cup which fastens to your belt. Encountering a mountain stream after hours of riding, we would dismount and dip our cups in the stream for what has to be the best-tasting drink in the world.

Just to set the record straight, let me explain that while I loved our ranch, I didn't share Ronnie's love for riding at that time and I have a fear of heights. I had some real trepidation about tackling horses and mountain tops when we set out on this trip, but I would not have backed out for anything in the world.

On the morning of our last day, we were riding a narrow trail, single file, with Ronnie in the lead and Ron bringing up the rear. There were only the sound of the wind in the tall pines, an occasional bird song, and the muffled beat of the horses' hooves on the soft pine needles. I will confess I was weary and saddlesore. Then I heard our son's voice, "Mom, you're doing all right. I really thought you'd last about one day and then find an excuse to go home." General Custer and the whole 7th Cavalry couldn't have driven me out of those mountains when I heard that.

That noon when we stopped for lunch (it happened to be my birthday, incidentally), Ron raised his Sierra cup and proposed a toast, announcing that he would have it engraved in his cup for me when we reached civilization. I treasure this cup, which is inscribed, "To The World's Greatest Camper—Sport—and Mom." Don't ask me how or why, but suddenly I was no longer weary and saddlesore. There must have been another effect, which I do not understand at all. As I told you, I am afraid of heights. That final afternoon we rode down into Yosemite Valley in Yosemite National Park. The trail was a narrow switchback cut into the side of a sheer 3,000-foot cliff. When we reached the valley floor, Ronnie turned around and asked if I was all right. I answered that I was, and why did he ask? He said, "Turn around and look up." I did, and for the first time realized where I had been.

Growing up in Chicago was of course completely different from what it would have been in Bethesda. I went to the Girls' Latin School and my brother went to the Boys' Latin School. The schools were separated by a few blocks but were joined by activities, dances, and the like. I was an average student but active in everything. I was president of my class a few times and of the Dramatic Club, where I acted in all of the plays. I played field hockey and basketball, and—still the romantic of all time —I always had a crush on someone. The schools had exchange dances, and an organization called the Fortnightly Club held a dance every two weeks. There were boys' football and basketball games to watch, so there was certainly no lack of social activity. In the summer I visited friends in Lake Geneva near Chicago, where we sailed, swam, and went to dances. My father was—and is—a good golfer and tried to get me interested in it, but he never really succeeded! I was more interested in tennis and swimming. Those were wonderfully happy days, and I remember them and all my friends with great affection.

After graduation from high school, I went to Smith College, a women's college in Northampton, Massachusetts. It was a long way from home, but I had longed to go there. Smith gave me an excellent general background and time, I hoped, in which to mature.

I originally intended to stay only a year or two, but I wound up staying all four years. I am very glad I did. During my first two years, I roomed with an old friend from Chicago, Jean Wescott, and the latter two years with Frannie Greene, who came from the east.

The biggest excitement during my time at Smith occurred because of a murder trial. A man was charged with killing his wife's lover. Of course, we were all intrigued, cut classes, and stood in line to get into the courthouse. I immediately cast the parts in my mind—the central characters would of course look like Cary Grant and Carole Lombard. Imagine my disappointment when a meek, short little man and his very fat wife came out of the courtroom. We all left, returned to class, and never went back. It seemed so sordid, instead of glamorous.

By today's standards, Smith was a small school of less than 2,500 students, but it seemed enormous to me. There were close to 250 teachers, which is a better-than-average ratio of teachers to students. We were close to our teachers and received a good education from them and the school.

I lived in an old off-campus house where I enjoyed life a great deal. Those were very happy and carefree days. The students were much less serious than they are today, much less politically involved. I knew nothing about politics. I don't say this with any pride, but it didn't seem important then.

I had a terrible time with science and math. My mind just did not seem to function correctly for these subjects. I majored in drama and did well. I had acted in high school plays, and I performed in college plays. When school was out, I was active in summer stock and playhouses in New England. It is lovely in New England, and I'm happy I had a chance to enjoy its lifestyle as I had those of New York, Chicago, and Bethesda, Maryland. At school in the fall we had "Mountain Day." We never knew when it would come until the chapel bells woke us at 7 A.M. That meant we had the whole day free to go out in the country, take a picnic, and really enjoy the vivid yellow and green leaves in the Berkshire Mountains, a truly breathtakingly beautiful sight.

I changed from a girl into a young woman during those years, but that time in my life was not without sadness. In those days girls made their debut, and I made mine at a tea dance at the Casino Club in Chicago. It was supposed to start at five o'clock in the evening. My family believed in punctuality, but others did not. At five o'clock few were there, and I was worried that few would come. The Princeton Triangle Club was in town (and had been invited) and were among the early arrivals. With the club this year was one Frank Birney. Seeing that I was nervous, he kept coming in and out and going up and down the line using a different name and accent and pretending he was a different boy just as if a whole crowd had arrived. He made me laugh. He made everyone laugh. He charmed everyone. Eventually, all the guests arrived.

After that episode, Frank and I started to see one another fairly steadily and seriously. I would go to Princeton for football games and dances, he would come to Smith for dances, or we would meet in New York for a weekend, "under the clock" at the Biltmore Hotel. Don't let that "for a weekend" statement fool you. It was different in those days. There was an all-girl floor at the Biltmore—no boys allowed! Frank and I went together for about eighteen months. We talked a little bit about getting married, but it ended in tragedy before that ever happened.

We were to meet in New York one weekend. I was waiting for him when the telephone call came. He was late and had hurried to catch the train at Princeton Junction and had jumped the gate to run across the tracks ahead of the oncoming train. The engineer saw him, but couldn't slow the train down in time. He was pulling the cord to the whistle so hard that it broke. Frank was killed instantly. After the funeral, his mother gave me a cigarette case I had had inscribed and given him for Christmas which he was carrying with him at the time.

While now I wonder whether I had really been in love with Frank or whether we would ever have married, it took me a long time to get over his death. I felt a deep loss then and a little scar still remains inside, but I learned that life goes on and you go on with it. I got back into college activities and eventually began to date again.

During my senior year in college, I started going quite seriously with a boy from Amherst College who lived in Massachusetts. Amherst was only seven miles from Smith, and the boys at Amherst and the Smith girls regularly saw each other for dances and other activities, and some began to go together. We saw quite a bit of each other during my senior year. When we graduated, the war was on, and we announced our engagement before he enlisted in the Navy.

It was a heady, exhilarating time, and I was swept up in the glamour of the war, wartime engagements, and waiting for the boys who were away. I realized I had made a mistake. It would have been unfair to him and to me. It wasn't easy to break off the engagement, but it was the best thing for us both. We were not meant to be married, but we remain friends to this day.

I almost feel I was fated to meet Ronnie. I cannot say I would not have married someone else if I had not met and married Ronnie, but I did meet him and I feel I was meant to marry him.

I have always been a romantic. I don't remember how Ronnie proposed because I think at some point when we were courting, we agreed we were going to get married and there was never a formal proposal. I did tell him once that I had not gotten the proposal of my dreams, in which he would take me out on a lake in a canoe, play a ukelele, sing to me, and propose as I was reclining with one hand drifting in the water. It became a joke between us, and I'm sure would be laughed at by today's generation. I had obviously seen that done in some movie and never forgot it.

On our twenty-fifth wedding anniversay, he gave me a canoe named *TruLuv* and took me out on the lake at our ranch. He did not have a ukelele, but I said it would be all right if he just hummed! It was a sentimental, sweet thing for him to do, and I loved it.

Maybe I am old-fashioned, but believing in true love, saving yourself for that true love, and having one husband for all of your life just seems to me how things should be, although I know it doesn't always work out that way. I feel about Ronnie as I never have felt about any other man. But I had my romances as does any young girl. And I think fondly about those few men I have known well in my life.

At Smith I had learned that life is not always easy, and romances do not always have romantic endings. I went through difficult changes and emotional experiences, and I learned that you have to take life as it comes and be prepared for sudden twists of fate. I learned that there are tears as well as laughs in life, tragedies and triumphs. And you have to make the most of every moment and the miracle of every morning.

Chapter 2

As I said before, Mother's stage career began very early. After she started working for her brother Joe, one of her first notices read,

> Little Edith Luckett has beauty, wit and talent. She is an unusual child. Her prattle is as merry as the chirp of the cricket on the hearth, her eyes blue and her hair wavy. She has been brought to public notice by her remarkable cleverness, her grace and her sweet, pretty face.

All those qualities plus others helped my wonderful mother on the way to her successful career. In New York she played with Nazimova in *'Ception Shoals*, George M. Cohan in *Broadway Jones*, and Spencer Tracy in *The Baby Cyclone*. In between these performances she was the leading lady of stock companies in Trenton, Pittsfield, Atlanta, and Dallas. They loved her. It's a joy to have her scrapbook and read for myself how much she was adored.

My godmother was Alla Nazimova. She was "Zim" to me but a legend to movie fans. Her home eventually became the famous Garden of Allah apartment complex where so many great performers and writers have stayed. Sad to say, years later she wound up living in just a small apartment in the Sunset Boulevard building that used to be her mansion. I came to know her better after I was out of college, when she was quite elderly. She was a great actress and a great lady.

Two of my mother's best friends were Walter and Nan Huston. He was Uncle Walter to me. His son John is now a famous director in his own right. I haven't seen John in many years, but I think of him almost as family. He calls my father often for medical advice. When Uncle Walter had an aneurism at the Beverly Hills Hotel, he asked John to call my father in Phoenix. My father caught the first plane for Hollywood, but, sadly, Uncle Walter died before he could get there.

Louis Calhern was also a close friend and would let no one but my father take care of him. On one occasion my father operated on Lou's spine to relieve a chronic back condition. Following the surgery, while he was being wheeled from the operating room, his heart stopped. My father lifted him from the stretcher, placed him on the floor, and began heart massage. Surgeons are faced with emergencies many times, but this was an especially traumatic experience for my father because he and Lou were such close friends. Possibly this is why surgeons prefer not to operate on friends or family, because of their emotional involvement. At any rate, my father refused to give up and was successful in reviving Lou. He never told Lou of his close brush with death.

Lou was stately and charming, but Spencer Tracy was the charmer of all time. Spence and Mother had been in stock together in Trenton, New Jersey, and he and his wife Louise were longtime family friends. He was a man of many moods, but when he smiled, it melted all hearts. In my opinion he was the greatest film actor ever.

Zasu Pitts, that fine, fluttery comedienne, another family friend, would in time give me my first professional opportunity as an actress.

As a child growing up with these greats of the entertainment world, I guess I took them for granted. I met Josh Logan and Jimmy Stewart at the Hustons and immediately had a big crush on Jimmy. Of course, I was aware of the great ability of these people, but for me they were, first and foremost, family friends, not stars.

While I was in high school, we spent our summers with the Hustons in the beautiful home they had built at Lake Arrowhead. It was far different from the Lake Arrowhead of today. There were only two other homes anywhere nearby, one owned by Hollywood's foremost agent, Myron Selznick, and the other by Reginald Denny, the actor. The only telephones available were at the general store and gas station farther down the mountain. I have some treasured photos and wonderfully warm memories of those days.

The mountains, with their great pine trees, were a magic land to a girl from the big city of Chicago. Uncle Walter's handsome house had a tennis court, swimming pool, and dining patio overlooking the mountains. He loved to make furniture, so there was a fully equipped workshop. Here my father even built two bedside tables—under Uncle Walter's supervision, of course.

We spent wonderfully lazy, carefree days playing tennis and swimming. I would take long walks in the woods in the afternoon, and in the evening we would either sit around the fire while Uncle Walter read to us, or go out and look through his telescope at the stars, which practically jumped out at you in those clear skies. When John was there, he and Uncle Walter had a game they played. It was a very simple one, which boiled down to which one could make the other laugh first. It was all done in pantomime. Neither one could speak, but they each would do the silliest, most outrageous thing to break the other one up. The first one who laughed lost the game, of course, but the rest of us were weak with laughter.

The place had a tree house called "Crovenay House." A painting of an eighteenth-century gentleman, bearing the nameplate "Alastair, duc de Crovenay," hung in the main house. Many thought this was a famous ancestor of the Huston family. The truth is the duke was counterfeit, a creation of Walter Huston's.

Uncle Walter started in vaudeville as a song-and-dance man in the days of the "five a day," meaning five performances a day. One night when he and a fellow performer returned to their hotel, they saw a man sitting in the lobby with a nondescript-looking dog. On impulse, Walter and his friend started loudly arguing over whether or not that "fine-looking dog" was a "pure-bred Crovenay."

Finally, they asked the man to settle the dispute—was the dog, in truth, a genuine "Crovenay"? As Uncle Walter tells it, the man, who had listened to the whole argument, said, "No, he isn't, but his mother was."

The following day, while on the train en route to their next booking, they asked a conductor, who was a loud, know-it-all type, if some ducks flying overhead were by any chance "Crovenays." He took a look out the window, then informed them, with a straight face, "Crovenays don't fly this far north."

Walter's sister, Margaret Jones, a well-known and respected dramatics teacher, was married to the scenic designer Robert Edmond Jones. One day she found a portrait in an antique store, had a brass nameplate made up for it, and the "duc de Crovenay" was born.

When Uncle Walter died, he left the portrait to my father, who, in turn, told its story to a delighted doctor friend, Daniel Collier Elkin. Together they formed the Crovenay Society, whose membership was limited to those who exposed know-it-all stuffed shirts.

One man gained membership by exposing a supposed expert on the growing of grass, a gentleman from Georgia who bored all his friends by constantly telling them what they were doing wrong with their lawns.

Describing a visit to a farm in Kentucky, the man informed the talkative expert of a new "bluer-than-bluer grass, hardier than rye," and, of course, it was called Crovenay. The expert said, "Oh, yes, I know it well, but it won't grow in Georgia."

Uncle Walter's friend, the great baseball immortal Ty Cobb, became a society member by way of a big-league scout who would have you believe he was the discoverer of more baseball talent than all of the other scouts in the game. Ty dreamed up an imaginary outfielder on a small-town team who, to hear him tell it, was the find of the century. There was, of course, no such player outside of Ty Cobb's mind.

The scout assured him he would take a look. The next time they met, Cobb asked him if he had seen the boy. The agent said he had and had really looked him over. He was great in the field, according to the agent, but, sad to say, he could not hit. "Crovenay" was only invoked by members of the club to puncture the pompous. My father was delighted to be a member of the club.

Once, Josh Logan came to Arrowhead to try to talk Uncle Walter into doing the stage play *Knickerbocker Holiday*. I sat with them by the pool while Josh read the play to all of us. Uncle Walter said he would think about it.

Afterward, he asked me if I thought he should do the role. He was a darling man, and I am sure now he just wanted me to feel that I was a part of the decision and that he valued my opinion. But, with the ego of youth, I assumed my opinion would be of great value to him. Since it was an offbeat part for him, I said, "Oh, Uncle Walter, I don't think it's right for you. I think it would be a big mistake for you to do it." He thanked me warmly for my counsel, but he also, without telling me, signed up to do the part.

Knickerbocker Holiday turned out to be a Broadway smash success and one of Walter Huston's most memorable performances. His singing of "September Song" made it a classic. Years later he sent me a book based on the production and impishly inscribed it, "To Nancy, who advised me to do this play?"

Walter Huston was a natural actor. He didn't have a dramatic manner. He didn't even read parts well. But whether on stage or screen, he brought widely varied characters to vivid life. In everyday life he did not show it, but he was a great instinctive actor. He received as much as $75,000 for a single screen performance when $75,000 was nearly top money in Hollywood. My father received only a fraction of that amount for performing brain surgery. Even though my father was a marvelous doctor, he refused to charge more than he felt patients could afford. We were comfortable but, of course, couldn't possibly live on the scale successful actors in the entertainment world could.

My father had the greatest respect and affection for Uncle Walter, but years later confessed he had often thought that men like him were overpaid. He felt that with his education and ability to read intelligently, he could easily do what Walter and other actors did. He certainly felt his own profession called for greater training. Of course, he kept such thoughts to himself and never in any way indicated this to Uncle Walter.

One day during one of our Arrowhead vacations, while Mother and Nan had gone into town to shop, Uncle Walter suggested we record a "radio broadcast." We would do a scene from a play as a surprise for the wives.

"It will be sponsored by the Crovenay Company, and Nancy Pantsy Davis can take part, too," Uncle Walter said. I was thrilled. So was my father. When the Hustons had played *Dodsworth* in Chicago, they had stayed with us. Father had frequently stood in the wings watching the last act while waiting to drive them home. He had almost memorized Uncle Walter's climactic speech.

Father asked Uncle Walter if he had a script of *Dodsworth* and volunteered to perform Walter's part in the final scene. Uncle Walter said he did indeed. Dad read that part, while I read Nan's part, which had been played on Broadway by Fay Bainter. I thought I did well, but my young girl's voice was no match for the mature voice of my father, who came off pretty well in the scene. This, of course, confirmed his belief that he was a natural actor. And even more so when Uncle Walter said we did well.

Then, with all of us keyed up, Walter suggested we do a scene from *Othello*. We were all for it. My father played Iago, I played Desdemona, and Uncle Walter played Othello, the role he had played on Broadway.

Uncle Walter wore a T-shirt, swimming trunks, and tennis shoes, but, as Father wrote some years later in his book *A Surgeon's Odyssey*, "Before our eyes he seemed to don robes, a ring appeared in his ears, his hair darkened and became curly, his skin became black." All this just while reading. With the magic of his art, he transformed himself into Othello before our eyes. The less said about Father's and my performances the better.

That night after dinner, Uncle Walter played the record for the ladies. The first performance passed. Mother and Nan praised my performance and especially Father's. Uncle Walter said, "No doubt about it, the kid was great. Now, we've got another one

62

for you." Played against the deep, dark power of Othello, my Desdemona sounded childish and Dad's Iago sounded foolish. The ladies laughed. They were easy on me but teased Father unmercifully. Mother told him, "You just got hammier and hammier." He took it with good nature. He was used to it.

Several days later, sitting by the pool, enjoying the warmth of the sun, the clear air, and the beauty of the mountains, Uncle Walter quietly turned to my father and said, "Kid, I always thought your job was easy. The first time I sat in the stands and watched you operate, I thought I could do it, too."

We all learned a lesson from that great man, who died suddenly in 1950 and whom I miss to this day. Uncle Walter had been aware all the time of what Father had been thinking, but never let him know it. When he did, he did so with great gentleness.

Growing up, I used to think about becoming an actress. I wanted to be like my mother. I loved seeing her on stage, and I loved being backstage and dressing up in her stage clothes and makeup.

As I look back on my life in Bethesda, I was always play-acting. I longed to be blond and have long curls. Finally, Mother in desperation bought me a Mary Pickford wig, thinking it would help. I wore it every chance I got and thought I was beautiful. I hesitate to think what the neighbors thought.

In college I majored in drama, of course. When I first went to Smith, Mr. Neilsen, who had been college President, had just retired. He was greatly loved and admired by everyone. Hallie Flanagan Davis had taken over as president as well as the head of the Drama Department, with Mr. McDowell as her assistant. The department was in a transition period, not well organized, but I gained some valuable acting experience, nonetheless.

The only production I remember in particular was a musical called *Banderlog*. I think it was the first time a musical had been performed at Smith. The department didn't discourage it, but it was the idea of the students. I played the lead, and it was the only time I sang and danced in any production. I didn't have to do anything extraordinary—nor did I——but it was fun and we all had a lot of enthusiasm.

The college had a small theater. Years later, when Ronnie was asked to be a Chubb Fellow at Yale for a week, I revisited Smith. There were no sororities, but when there I lived in Talbot House, one of the old residential houses. I went back to my old house and my old room and stirred up marvelous memories. I had lunch with the president and others on the staff, and they took me to their new theater, which was one of the most elaborate, beautiful theaters I have ever seen. In a strange way, I was not happy with it, and when they asked me, I told them, "I think it's beautiful, but I've always believed we should strive to go up. So I hope you warn anyone interested in going on in drama that after this they have nowhere to go but down, as far as facilities are concerned."

By far the best theatrical experience I received in those days was in the rickety old summer-stock theaters on the eastern seaboard. The one I remember best was in Bass Rocks, Massachusetts. The theater was run by Martin Manulis and Henry Levin. We all ended up in California finally. As a matter of fact, Marty's children and mine went to school together later.

As was customary, the theater had a resident company with apprentices, of which I was one. The producers brought in guest stars, and it depended on how large a company these stars brought with them how many of our group performed in the productions. My first summer I had only one part, and my line was—believe it or not—"Dinner is served." It is like an old show-business joke, but true.

As an apprentice, I did everything—painted scenery, upholstered furniture, ran errands, tacked up announcements in the town, cleaned dressing rooms, and so forth. I learned a lot about the actors from the way in which they left their dressing rooms. Some couldn't have cared less about the condition of their rooms and the fact that others would occupy them after they left. Others were clean, calm, and neat people, whose performances were as orderly as their dressing rooms.

One can learn a great deal just by watching skilled directors and talented stars at work. When I wasn't working, I took advantage of sitting in on every rehearsal I could. The directors from those days that I remember best were Josh Logan and Antoinette Perry. Josh I knew as a family friend. The Tony awards, which are Broadway's Oscars, were named for Antoinette.

These creative people knew what they wanted from each production, and they could inspire the performers to make the most of their budding abilities. I don't think young players today have such opportunities to learn their craft. In my day there were many stock companies in which you could do apprentice work and learn. If you were lucky enough to be signed by a Hollywood studio, the studio management built and guided your career slowly and gave you the needed publicity. Today, young people are more or less left on their own to sink or swim, it seems to me, with no real direction, and many times their careers are over before one is even aware they started.

One summer, Buddy Ebsen was one of the visiting stars appearing in *The Male Animal.* I had charge of the offstage and intermission music. I had a big crush on Buddy, and one night I became so engrossed with the play that I forgot to put the record on when he went over to the Victrola on stage. Dead silence. Buddy started to ad-lib, and it finally dawned on me what had happened. I fumbled around and after what seemed like hours, I finally rushed the record on. I thought he never would forgive me and dissolved in tears, but he was an understanding man. He followed me outside and told me it was all right, not to worry, and the world was brighter again.

Summer stock was a memorable experience, and so I decided to pursue a stage career. However, when I graduated from Smith, World War II was on. My father was serving overseas, and my mother was alone. She had no need for our big apartment, so she sublet it and moved into the Drake Hotel. I came home to move in with her until the war ended and my father returned.

I wanted to work to make some money and keep myself occupied. While studying to be a nurse's aide, I worked in the college shop at Marshall Field, a large department store in downtown Chicago. My most unforgettable experience there was catching a shoplifter. A woman was circling around a display case in the center of the floor, and I looked up just in time to see her put a piece of jewelry in her purse. I looked around for the store detective, for anyone, but no one was available. I went up to the woman and asked if I could be of help to her. She said, No, she was just looking. She asked the price of some gloves at the top of the display. I looked up and said, "Seven ninety-five"—it could have been two ninety-five or twenty-five ninety-five for all I knew, I wasn't about to take my eyes off her.

No one had really prepared me for what to do in such an emergency. She started to leave and I was frantic. As calmly as possible, I said, "Don't you think you better give me back the jewelry before you go?" Whereupon she broke away and started to run for the elevator, with me hot on her heels. When I think about it now, we must have made quite a sight. The store detective appeared miraculously from nowhere, and the woman was stopped at the elevator. She turned, took hold of the top of my button-down dress, and tore it right down the front. The detective took both of us and hustled us to the store offices. Here he found that her shopping bags were full of loot she had lifted from this and other stores.

I had to tell the whole story, all the while certain this woman was putting some kind of curse on me as she glared at me. They sent me away, and I think the police came to take her away, though I am not sure. Later, I was reprimanded for stopping the shoplifter in the store. I learned that you have to wait until a shoplifter has left a store to substantiate the charge that the customer had no intention of paying for whatever was taken. I was given a twenty-five-dollar check as a reward, and even though I had gone about it all wrong, I was very proud! Still, I must say I enjoyed my volunteer work at the hospital during the evening more than my paid duties at the store during the day.

My father came home shortly before the war ended because he was ill. We moved back into our apartment, and soon a call came from Zasu Pitts. I suspect that Mother had a hand in it. Zasu told me there was a part available for me in a play she had on tour, *Ramshackle Inn*. That first part is the hardest to get.

Until then, when producers or casting directors or agents ask you what you have done, you can only speak of college plays or summer stock. When you get your first part in a professional production, then you have a credit. I grabbed the offer and joined the company in Detroit, where the girl who had been playing the part was leaving. I played the role of a girl who has been held captive in an upstairs room. At one point, I came downstairs, spoke my three lines, and was returned to my room. It wasn't much but it was a start, and I was out on my own with the best wishes of my parents.

I wasn't exactly alone. I was more than a family friend to Zasu. She had a daughter, Ann, whom she missed very much. In a way, I took her place. Zasu insisted I share her dressing rooms and hotel rooms, which I was happy to do. It was a brand-new world to me and, not being used to the road, having a friend was very comforting. Zasu had been a great beauty in her youth and at this point in her career looked ageless. Actually, she was only in her late forties and a great comedienne. She was also a darling lady and took good care of me. We traveled with the play across country and wound up in New York playing the "subway circuit." We played theaters in Brooklyn, Long Island, The Bronx, and so forth.

I settled into New York, although later in the fall of 1946, Zasu helped me get a part in another of her plays, *Cordelia*, which played Boston, Hartford, and other New England cities. Unlike the song—they did not hang a star on my dressing-room door. I was hardly noticed in my first play, but received good notices in my second.

Back in New York, clippings in hand, I made the rounds of producers' offices, casting agencies, and tryouts. It was a long time between jobs. Fortunately, I wasn't entirely alone in the big city. When I was living on East 51st Street, the Hustons had an apartment around the corner. Lillian Gish, another family friend, had one nearby. They often took me out to eat or to a show, or had me over to little parties. I used to go watch Spence rehearse for a play he was opening in, *The Rugged Path*. He was very nervous about returning to the stage, but he was very good, as he always was.

After he returned to Hollywood, the Tracys sent their son John to stay with me for a while. John was the inspiration for the John Tracy Clinic, which was started by Louise Tracy and still endures, doing important work for the deaf. John had been born deaf. He also had extremely poor eyesight and had had polio—so much affliction for one boy. His parents had always tried to teach him that he could do whatever he wanted to do. After he graduated from college, he wanted to visit New York. They didn't want to discourage him, so they suggested he stay with me and asked if I would look after him, and I agreed. He stayed with me less than a week, yet the experience left a deep impression on me. He slept in the living room on a couch that opened up into a bed. I took him to art museums and even to the theater. He enjoyed musicals. Somehow, he sensed the music through the vibrations he felt.

There was a girl John wanted to take to dinner and dancing. He had met her when she visited California, and he made a date with her. I was concerned because of his difficulty in communicating. Without telling him, I made a phone call and explained the problem in advance to the hotel maitre d' and hoped for the best. John became very excited as the night drew near. That day, the girl called in sick to cancel the date. I could tell she wasn't ill, she just did not want to go out with Johnny. It had been one thing to meet Spencer Tracy's son and therefore meet Spence in Hollywood; it was another thing to date his handicapped son in New York. Well, she was a lot more handicapped than he as far as I was concerned. I took the telephone call, turned away from Johnny so he couldn't read my lips, and told her what I thought of her leading him on. I was furious at her and so sad for him.

I tried to soften the blow, but he was hurt. I went out for dinner and dancing with him as his date, and we had a good time. He was a marvelous young man, and I admired his courage enormously. His parents and his sister Suzie helped him, and he helped himself. In time, he married and had a child and, though he later became divorced, he managed to make a life for himself. I remember the night he left me in New York. A representative from MGM came to take him to the airport. The man took one of his two bags, and I started to take the other to help him down to the car. He said, "Oh, no, you're my princess and I'm your slave," and took his own bag. I kissed him good-bye and dissolved into tears.

I dated men in and out of show business while I lived in New York. I knew a lot of actors as friends, but I dated more writers and directors than actors, and a lot more assistant directors and assistant producers than directors and producers. We were young people trying to make it in the theater and were thrown together a lot, but I had no serious romances.

Through Spence, I had some dates with an actor who was known affectionately as "The King." Clark Gable was coming to New York—it was summer and I guess everyone he knew was out of town. So Spence gave him my number, then got cold feet and called Mother to tell her what he had done. Mother phoned to warn me that if someone called saying he was Clark Gable, I must not answer, "Yes, and I'm Greta Garbo." She was right to warn me because that's just what I would have done!

He traveled by train, called when he arrived and asked me to dinner. I lived in a walk-up apartment, and I couldn't picture Clark Gable walking up three flights of stairs to date an unknown young actress, but he did. The World Series was in town, and we discovered we both liked baseball. So we would go every day, then have dinner and perhaps go to the theater or the Stork Club, which was the place to go in those days.

I knew all sorts of stars as family friends, but Gable was Gable, The King. It was my first experience going anywhere with a star of that magnitude. When we went to the theater, everyone would stand and not sit down again until he waved his hand. Trying to get out of the theater or ball game required a lot of police cooperation. At restaurants all heads would turn to look at him. He had incredible charisma. I was completely unprepared for all of this attention, and I got the impression he was a little embarrassed by it, too. I suspect, like Spence, he was never really comfortable with his stardom.

Although he didn't like parties, we did go to one. I was sure I would be forgotten and left in a corner somewhere when some of the gorgeous and famous glamour girls got to him. They were

were certainly aware of his presence! But nothing like that happened. When he was with you, he was with you and only you, and never looked over your shoulder to see who else was in the room. I think the secret of his charm was that he made whoever he was with feel important. He made me feel important, and I must say it gave my ego a boost. The fan magazines and gossip columns made a lot of it for awhile, but there never was any real romance between us. I think Mother became a little concerned though after reading a few items in the paper, because one day she called and after a lot of throat clearing, finally asked, "Nancy, what's going on?"

By and large, however, my life in New York in the late 1940's was no glamorous whirl of handsome escorts and wild night life. It was making the rounds of agencies and trudging to tryouts. Tryouts are the most difficult part of the profession. You don't know your part. You don't have time to rehearse it. You don't play it to an audience. You read in front of highly critical people who may not be sure what they want.

Tryouts are frightening and embarrassing. There are excellent actors and actresses who do not do well, and there are some highly successful performers who say they have never gotten a part as a result of a tryout. But if you are beginning in the theater and your ability is not established, you have no choice but to try out. And even if you pass, you remain on trial. There is a period after a show goes into rehearsal when many performers are replaced. In the days when I was in the theater, the first five days of rehearsal were critical. You could be fired at any time during that period and not be paid.

I got a part in one play on the basis of a tryout, but I was fired after a few days. I don't even remember the name of the play or the director. Maybe I don't want to remember. I do recall that when we broke for lunch during the rehearsal, the director caught up with me, took my arm, and led me out the stage door into the alley. "I hate to have to tell you this," he said, "but it's just not working. You're just not right for the part. I have to let you go."

Maybe I wasn't right for the part. Or maybe I just wasn't any good. We cannot all be right for every part on the stage or in life. We cannot all be good at everything. But I found out how painful it is to be rejected. It was the first and last time I was ever fired from anything and it hurt horribly. I was so embarrassed. I begged the director to go back to the dressing room to get my coat and purse as I did not want to face the other people in the show. Even if they did not yet know I had been fired, they would know soon enough. I did not want them to see me leaving. He brought me my coat and purse, and I left, humiliated and depressed.

It has happened to the best of performers, but when it happens to you, you begin to think that perhaps you aren't good enough and shouldn't go on. You lose your confidence and have to push yourself to go on. Unless you have an enormous ego that makes you feel you are right and everyone else is wrong, you really have to want something very much not to give up. My ego wasn't that big, but I did not want to quit, so I mustered what courage I could and hung on. I was saved by landing a part in a new show which became a hit on Broadway.

Making the rounds again, I went up to Michael Myerberg's office and read for a part in a play he was producing. After all of the tryouts, readings, refusals, and waiting for refusals by telephone, it was unbelievable how swift and easy it was when I heard the magic words, "You've got the part."

The show was a musical, *Lute Song*, with Mary Martin and Yul Brynner. Mary was an established star of the musical theater, while Yul was getting his first major opportunity. They were marvelous. Mary became a close and dear friend, which she is to this day. Yul was a charming man, and all of the ladies in the company had crushes on him. By the way, he had hair on his head at that time.

I played an Oriental, Tsi Chun, though I am not sure how the name is spelled, and I had to dye my hair black. It was not a big part, but it was a good one and I received good reviews. We opened in New Haven and Boston before bringing the play to New York, where it ran for about six months. How exciting it was to finally be playing on Broadway!

That was in 1946—a big year for the Broadway theater. The

71

Old Vic Theatre Company brought Laurence Olivier and Ralph Richardson over from London to perform classics that season. The big new American hit was *Born Yesterday*, with Judy Holliday and Paul Douglas. Ethel Merman also had a smash musical, *Annie Get Your Gun*.

There were many more hit shows, but, sad to say, there is nothing quite like them these days on Broadway, and I find myself wondering if there ever will be again. The great show people still perform occasionally and a great dramatic or musical play still surfaces from time to time, but there is nothing that approaches the variety of performer and play we had in the heyday of Broadway theater, and I feel fortunate to have been around then.

Lute Song played the Plymouth Theater. *Three to Make Ready* played an adjoining theater. When I was not due on stage, I would go over to watch Gordon MacRae, Ray Bolger, and Arthur Godfrey in *Three to Make Ready*. MacRae and two other friends of mine in New York, Pat Neal and Jean Hagen, later wound up with me at Metro-Goldwyn-Mayer in Hollywood.

I had a long break in the second act and would go down and sit with the doorman Jack Warren to pass the time. He was a dear, and often had coffee and sweet rolls ready for our nightly chats. Years later, when he was in his eighties, he came out to California to visit me after I was married to Ronnie. When I think back on the life I led in the theater, brief and minor as it may have been, I think of the many friends I made, few of whom were stars.

When *Lute Song* closed in New York, Mary Martin left the cast and Dolly Haas took the play on tour. I could have gone on the road with it, but instead took a new part with my old friend Zasu Pitts in *Cordelia*, which was in tryouts out of town and was supposed to make it to Broadway, but never did. I wound up on the road with Zasu in the George Abbott production of *The Late Christopher Bean*, which played Chicago and enabled me to have a reunion with my family.

I still have the reviews of these plays. I was young and usually played ingenue roles. I was described as "a sweet and decorous girl" in one and as "unusually attractive and talented" in another.

72

Here is "The Gipper" in his first A picture, *Knute Rockne: All American.*

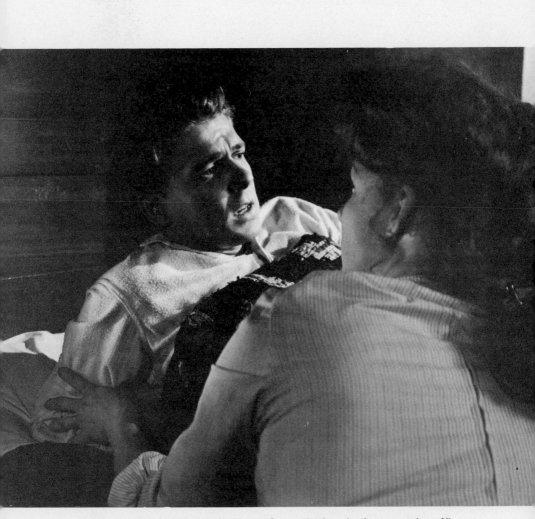

In *King's Row* Ronnie is asking, "Where's the rest of me?"

My first movie, *Shadow on the Wall*, with Ann Sothern (above), Gigi Perreau, and John McIntyre (below).

Then I played in *The Doctor and the Girl* with Gloria De Haven, Glenn Ford, and Charles Coburn.

In *East Side, West Side* with Barbara Stanwyck.

With Jim Whitmore in *The Next Voice You Hear*, the movie that Dore Schary expected Bill Wellman to make in seven days.

Bill Wellman, the lion who turned out to be a pussycat.

Night into Morning with Ray Milland and John Hodiak may have been my best picture.

It was a thrill playing opposite this leading man in *It's a Big Country*.

With Jim Whitmore again and Ralph Meeker in *Shadow in the Sky*.

In *Talk About a Stranger* I played George Murphy's wife and Billy Gray's mother.

I costarred with Lew Ayres in *Donovan's Brain*, a film that must have amused my father. It was good to have an occasional visit on the set from my husband (right).

In *Rescue at Sea* I played opposite Gary Merrill. It was a film that is best forgotten.

In my last film, *Hellcats of the Navy*, I had the pleasure of being my husband's fiancée.

—PHOTO BY CRONENWETH

Ronnie with the photos of some of the stars who acted in General
Electric Theater on television.

One notice read, "Nancy Davis gave a good account of herself." Naturally, I was pleased and I treasured every word, but I wasn't setting show business on fire. However, I honestly don't think I even thought of that. I was doing something I wanted to do and having a good time.

Chapter 3

Back in New York, I did a little television. I had performed on one television show in Chicago, but all I remember about it is that I had to wear green makeup and black lipstick. You had to wear a lot of odd colors to look close to normal on the black-and-white television cameras of those days. In New York I did the play *Ramshackle Inn* with Zasu, and then something called *Broken Dishes*. I don't remember much about the story line of *Broken Dishes*, but it turned out to be one of the most important parts I ever played. Someone from Metro saw me in it and called my agent, who phoned and said they wanted me to come out to the coast to test for a movie contract. I started packing before I hung up the phone.

This was one opportunity that none of my family friends had anything to do with, but when I called Mother to tell her the news, she telephoned Spence. He arranged to have George Cukor direct my test, which was a break for me. George Cukor was—and is—one of the best directors in Hollywood. He was also kind and understanding. I was proud that I'd gotten the opportunity on my own, but not too proud to accept help to make the most of it.

I tested with Howard Keel, who had just been signed at Metro. George Folsey, a great cameraman, photographed the scene. I never saw the test, but I must have passed because I was offered the usual contract for starters—seven years with options. The options, of course, were the studio's. Metro could drop me, but I couldn't drop them, and they paid $250 a week to start. I grabbed it. That was in the summer of 1949—a year that marked the end of one period of life and the beginning of another.

Louis B. Mayer was head of MGM at that time. The studio still had stars under long-term contracts. Spence, Gable, Fred Astaire, Judy Garland, Ava Gardner, Elizabeth Taylor, Lana Turner, June Allyson, and a hundred others were working on the Metro lot in Culver City. The era of the big studios and the star system had not yet ended.

Spence appeared in two big pictures in 1949: *Edward, My Son* with Deborah Kerr and *Adam's Rib* with Katie Hepburn and Judy Holliday. Astaire and Ginger Rogers did their last picture together, *The Barkleys of Broadway*. Kelly and Sinatra made *Take Me Out to the Ball Game*. Jimmy Stewart and June Allyson did the baseball picture *The Stratton Story*. Uncle Walter worked with Gregory Peck and Ava Gardner in *The Great Sinner*.

It was a great time and few if any of us were aware it would not last much longer. The stability of the business had been wrecked when the government ruled that the major studios could no longer own theaters. Television was making deep inroads, and the great studios were beginning to make fewer films. Without their own theaters to showcase the films they made, the studios could no longer afford to keep high-priced talent under long-term contract, and soon the big stars would go out on their own. Some would end up making money freelancing, but a lot of lesser performers would lose their livelihood. A great work force of people who put pictures together would find themselves out of work, and what has been called the Golden Era of pictures would come to an end.

But that was yet to come. I was thrilled to be a part of Hollywood, which was still a spectacular industry. I hadn't had enough confidence in my chances of success to give up my apartment in New York when I left to take the test, but after I signed a contract, I returned to New York to pack up my belongings and headed for Hollywood to stay. I took a small house in Santa Monica at first, then later moved into an apartment on Beverly Glen. Van and Evie Johnson lived down the street from me in Santa Monica. We all used to get together on Sundays and play tennis and swim. It was a small, dead-end street, and everyone knew each other.

I was terribly nervous when I took my screen test, but in time I found films easier than plays. With the camera on you, you don't have to exaggerate as you do on the stage, where even a facial reaction must be recognized in the very last row. It was always much easier for me to do a one-on-one performance, where I could be more subtle in my relationship with the other actors. With every scene set apart from every other one, I found that you can concentrate on each one and redo it as often as necessary to bring out the best that is in you.

It is said that the stage demands greater talent, but I think great talent prevails in any medium. Some actors may be better suited to one medium or another, but both stage and film are equally demanding.

I wasn't a superstar, nor—in the company of an Elizabeth Taylor, an Ava Gardner, a Lana Turner—could I conceivably be considered a great beauty. But I managed not to break any cameras, and, as it turned out, I didn't have the time to discover whether I could ever join the upper galaxy. In those first months I mostly played a series of roles in which I was either a young wife with children or about to have a child. I was padded to appear pregnant more times than I can recall, but at least I escaped the usual starlet and bathing-suit routine.

I made eight films in four years before I married Ronnie. I appeared in only four films in the following four years, the last one with Ronnie, before I made good my determination to retire from movie-making for good so I could be the wife I wanted to be. I made eleven films in all from 1949 through 1956, and I had to look up a lot of them before I could remember much about them. It's really like talking about another life.

However, I can remember going into the makeup department for my first day of shooting and how exciting it was for me to be sitting next to June Allyson or Elizabeth Taylor, both of whom later became good friends. Sidney Guilaroff was the famous hair stylist, and Bill Tuttle was head of makeup. As I was being made up the first day, Bill came in to introduce himself and said, "Well, I guess that's all right, but we'll have to do something about her eyes—they're too big for pictures." He was joking, but I was so nervous I thought he was serious, so I went around the rest of the day with my eyes half closed. Finally, George Folsey took me aside and asked me if I was tired, what was the matter? I told him what Bill Tuttle had said, and I thought he'd never stop laughing. Finally, wiping the tears from his eyes, he said, "Nancy, don't you know your eyes can never be too big for pictures?" He had Bill Tuttle come down to the set to confirm the fact he was joking before I'd really believe him and open my eyes again.

I think the first movie I made was *Death in a Doll's House* with Zachary Scott, Ann Sothern, and Gigi Perreau, but it was retitled *Shadow on the Wall* and wasn't released until the spring of 1950. I made *Bodies and Souls*, which became *The Doctor and the Girl*, with Glenn Ford, and, later, *East Side, West Side* with Barbara Stanwyck, but they were released earlier, late in 1949.

A lot of movies were made in those days, and it was not uncommon to hold different ones for different release dates, depending on other pictures that were coming out at about the same time. For example, a star might make two movies in rapid succession, but the studios didn't want both films playing at the same time, so they'd hold one back.

Because it was my first movie, I was naturally scared doing *Shadow on the Wall*, but Zachary Scott and Ann Sothern were seasoned professionals who went out of their way to be supportive and encouraging to me. In my limited career, I found this wasn't unusual. Players were supportive of other players and professional in attitude and conduct, even the biggest stars. Oh, there were a few temperamental ones who demanded special attention, didn't know their lines, or had drinking problems—but only a few.

Pat Jackson, an Englishman, directed *Shadow*. He helped me a lot and made my transition from stage to film fairly easy. After all, my experience as an actress in any medium was limited and I had to find my way, so I was grateful for any help I could get. Thank Heaven I wasn't a so-called Method actress and didn't have to imagine myself a tomato in order to play a scene that called for me to eat a salad. There is a fine line in acting, and I've never heard of a textbook that can define that line. You play the character the writer has created, but you also play the role partly the way you yourself would react in a given situation.

The Doctor and the Girl was Glenn Ford's first film for Metro. It also starred Charles Coburn, Bruce Bennett, Janet Leigh, and Gloria DeHaven. Coburn and Ford played doctors. Coburn was the father, and Glenn, Gloria, and I were his children. Janet played Glenn's wife.

East Side, West Side was an outstanding picture, starring Ava Gardner, Cyd Charisse, Van Heflin, and James Mason, as well as Barbara Stanwyck. I appeared in only a part of the film but my one big scene was with Barbara. I was nervous working with a star of her reputation and especially so because I had to give a long speech. But when I got it right on the first take, she applauded and congratulated me, which of course made me feel marvelous.

However, *East Side, West Side*, like the play *Broken Dishes*, is memorable for something other than my performance in it. While we were filming it, the director, Mervyn LeRoy, introduced me to an actor, a fellow over at Warner Brothers named Ronald Reagan. I'll get back to that a little later.

I received good reviews for my early films, which was a relief. I didn't know if I was good or bad, but I remember getting my first fan letter. I was so excited when they gave it to me that I pinned it on the front of my dress and wore it around the studio. Unless you were a star, you weren't often invited to see the "rushes." These were prints of each day's shooting that were run in a projection room at the end of each day's work. Sometimes they bent the rules and let me watch. Some actors prefer not to see them, but I found them very helpful and instructive.

Then, of course, there were the sneak previews when the finished picture was run unannounced in a theater to obtain audience reaction. My first such preview was at the Bay Theater in Pacific Palisades near where we now live, and I found, along with everyone else, that you really look only at yourself and it's a terrifying experience. You can't believe that's really you on that big screen, and you're sure you don't sound like that!

I did well enough to test for the female part in the film version of Louis Calhern's stage success *The Magnificent Yankee*. I am told I did well, but I didn't get the part. It was just as well. While I would have liked to have worked with Lou, the role was a difficult one which called for the character to age considerably as the picture went on. I wasn't ready for that sort of challenge.

By this time Dore Schary had succeeded Louis B. Mayer as head of MGM and was going to produce a picture called *The Next Voice You Hear*. They had cast Jim Whitmore in the husband's part, but were searching for the girl to play his wife. This was a pet project of Dore's. In the story the action took place over seven days, and Dore wanted it shot in seven days. Monday's action was shot on Monday, Tuesday's on Tuesday, and so forth. This, of course, was very different from the usual Metro pictures, which had long shooting schedules and were quite expensive (not by today's standards though!). I tested for Jim's pregnant wife and got the part. In the movie, for six straight days God's voice interrupted radio programs all over the world. By the seventh day—Sunday—everyone on earth was glued to a set awaiting his voice, which didn't come on. I remember Jimmy had a line, "I guess he's resting." I wasn't. That was the day I gave birth to my first baby—on screen, that is.

William Wellman directed the film, and I was nervous because I'd heard he was strictly a man's director and hated directing women. But he was a tiger who turned out to be a pussycat, even though he was known as "Wild Bill Wellman." I remember Bill didn't want me to wear any makeup in the film or to have a hairdresser. He wanted everything in the film as natural as possible.

I did what he wanted, and he helped me make the most of my part. He was a marvelous man and we became very good friends. I absolutely adored him.

Jim Whitmore and I worked well together, and we also became good friends. The studio liked the way we worked, and we were teamed again in 1952—he as a shell-shocked war veteran and I as his wife—in *Rain, Rain Go Away*, which became *Shadow in the Sky*, also starring Ralph Meeker and my late friend, Jean Hagen. Jean found fame later in life as the wife of Danny Thomas in television's *Make Room for Daddy*.

The Next Voice You Hear, which came out in the summer of 1950, opened at Radio City Music Hall in New York. What a thrill that was, seeing my name on the long marquee wrapped half-way around that great theater. Metro sent me to New York to promote the film, and I can remember stopping the car so that I could get out and gaze at my name up there. I couldn't believe it. They took a picture of it, which I still have.

It was an unusual film and, as a result, was highly publicized. Possibly because of all the publicity, it didn't quite live up to expectations. Still, it attracted a lot of attention and while not breaking any box-office records, it did all right, I think, and I know it did all right by me. My name now went above the title.

A year later, *Night Into Morning* opened. This movie was originally entitled *People in Love* and starred Ray Milland, John Hodiak, and me, along with Jean Hagen and Lewis Stone. I had a good part, and it may well have been the best picture I ever did. The film was shot on a college campus. I played John's fiancée, one of the few times I wasn't a wife. I had known Johnny when he worked in radio in Chicago. Now he was a rising star in pictures. Tragically, like Jean Hagen he died young, much too young.

Ray Milland, of course, was wonderful to work with—an Academy-Award winner and established star. It was exciting to do so many scenes with him throughout the picture.

But it was a scene with Johnny I'll always remember. John Hodiak was a very serious young man. You didn't think of him as suited to comedy roles, and I don't believe I ever heard him tell a joke.

97

We filmed a scene on a local university campus, in which we had to walk down a long flight of steps toward the camera. As we approached the camera, John was supposed to be laughing uproariously (not an easy thing for him to do).

Well, we made take after take. One time something would be wrong with the camera, another time the sound man would be dissatisfied—things just kept going wrong. Up the stairs we'd go again, and they seemed to be getting steeper each time. But, worst of all, Johnny was running out of laughs. On the next take, his attempt to muster a laugh produced a hollow cackle that was far from uproarious.

The director gave some excuse as to why we had to do it again, then took me aside and said, "You've got to think of something funny to say to him to make him laugh." This was a frightening assignment—you just can't come up with a funny line when you're told to.

We started down the steps, my mind a complete blank. Looking at Johnny, I knew he didn't have even a chuckle left inside of him. We were almost within microphone range and I was desperate. At the last possible second, out of the corner of my mouth I whispered, "Belly button." We took one more step and, suddenly, deadpan Johnny howled with laughter. The director said, "Cut and print that one." I basked in his gratitude for days.

Early in 1952, *It's a Big Country* was released. It was a big picture, made up of many different episodes. It starred Gary Cooper, Fredric March, William Powell, Gene Kelly, George Murphy, Van Johnson, Janet Leigh, Ethel Barrymore, and others. Another of Dore Schary's pet projects, it was supposed to show "the American way of life" in nine episodes, which were eventually cut to seven.

Different directors directed different episodes. I played opposite Freddie March in a segment I believe was called "Four Eyes." Freddie played an Italian immigrant who could not see that his son needed eyeglasses. I played a schoolteacher. Freddie was one of the great stars, maybe the greatest I ever played opposite, and he was a real pro. I wish the segment could have been a whole picture. I'm sure I could have learned a lot from him.

That year also saw the release of my second costarring film with Jim Whitmore, *Shadow in the Sky*, and one in which I costarred with George Murphy, *Talk About a Stranger*. In this movie I played Murph's wife. We both did it as a favor to the studio. Neither of us has ever seen it because it turned out to be as bad as we thought it would be when we read the script. We often threaten each other with getting a print and running it, but neither of us has the nerve.

Talk About a Stranger was also my last film at MGM. I married Ronnie in 1952 and wanted to quit acting, but I was talked into a few films after that. One was *Donovan's Brain*, which I made in 1954 with Lew Ayres. I remember he told me he enjoyed working with me because I listened to his lines. Many performers are so concerned with themselves they don't bother to listen to their costars.

I never got a lot of advice from the great actors I knew as family friends, but I remember Spence Tracy telling me, "Learn your lines, but listen to the other fella's lines, too," and I heeded this advice. Uncle Walter's contribution was "Try not to bump into the furniture." I tried to heed that advice also.

Donovan's Brain was science fiction. The brain of a criminal is kept alive and eventually takes over the scientist, who was played by Lew Ayres. It was silly, of course, but it was popular and is still shown on television now and then. Considering his profession, my father must have found it pretty funny.

Ronnie also found something pretty funny in *Donovan's Brain*, but it wasn't in the script. Not many people realize that glamorous Hollywood is sometimes a place of early to bed and even earlier to rise when you are shooting a picture. One day the schedule called for me to arrive early enough in the makeup and wardrobe departments so that all those chores could get done in time to travel to an outdoor location quite a distance from the studio. This meant leaving home at four-thirty in the morning. Since it was winter, this was quite long before sunrise and the streets were very empty. Driving through Beverly Hills on my way to the studio, I suddenly saw a flashing red light in my rearview mirror. Dutifully pulling over to the curb, I waited for an officer to tell me what section of the motor-vehicle code I'd violated.

The squad car pulled up behind me, and not one but two officers got out. They approached me, one on either side of my car. I handed the nearest officer my driver's license without waiting to be asked. He gave it a quick look and handed it back. I asked what I'd done and he didn't answer. He began questioning me about where I'd been, where I was going, etc., while his partner on the other side of the car pointed a flashlight around in the back seat, on the floor, and then on the floor in front. It was all very strange, I thought, but eventually they sent me on my way without even telling me why they'd stopped me.

When I got home that night, I told Ronnie about it and how puzzling the whole thing had been. He began to smile, and as I continued describing my adventure, he started to laugh. Then, very gently, he pointed out that the officers, seeing a young lady in a nice-looking convertible wheeling through town at that hour, quite possibly thought I might be a girl on her way home from a particular kind of work, not one on her way to work.

Donovan's Brain was released in 1954. I also did *Rescue at Sea*, which may have appeared as *The Frogman* in 1955, if it came out at all. I played opposite Gary Merrill, and it's another picture I'd just as soon forget. Every performer has a few of these in the closet. Ronnie calls them "pictures the studio didn't want good—it wanted them Thursday."

Finally I made *Hellcats of the Navy*, which came out in 1956. This one I did with Ronnie and it was my last film. I did it because it was a chance to be in a movie with him. We were married, but I played his fiancée in the film, which was the story of an actual submarine operation in World War II, whose code name had been "Operation Hellcat."

What I remember best is a scene in which Ronnie is about to go to sea in his submarine and we say farewell. The scene was shot on a dock in San Diego in front of a stack of explosive mines. I was sending him off to risk his life and I couldn't stand it. The idea got to me. I kept breaking up in tears, and we had to reshoot and reshoot. However, I must say the love scenes in this film were the easiest I ever had to do.

* * *

Aside from a few parts opposite Ronnie when he hosted and occasionally acted in the General Electric Theater on television, this was the last acting I did. I had no desire to continue as an actress once I became a wife. The whole idea of simultaneously pursuing a career and being a wife is a very personal and individual choice. I had seen too many marriages fall apart when the wife continued her career. I knew it wouldn't be possible for me to have the kind of marriage I wanted—and Ronnie wanted, though he never asked me to give it up—if I continued my acting career.

Acting is very demanding, by its nature somewhat self-centered, and it's easy for that attitude to slide over into a marriage. I think marriage is a full-time job and in these situations, either the marriage or the career suffers, usually the marriage. I'm sure some people have done it successfully, but I just didn't want to take that risk. Ronnie and I had both been burned before, so to speak, and I wanted everything going for me.

I must say acting was good training for the political life which lay ahead for us. We were accustomed to the crowds, interviews, and demands that stardom makes. There are tremendous pressures in both the theater and politics. The public sees only the glamorous side; but, oh, to see from the inside the perils that prominence can bring and how difficult it can be to deal with. Many famous performers have found success not sweet at all; I have seen some of their difficulties and have been saddened.

Actors may find fame and fortune in films, but they don't always find happiness. I think you have to be very stable and have had a firm grounding on what's important in life in order to handle either the acting profession or politics. If success comes suddenly and you're not prepared for it, you're bound to have difficulty dealing with it. It can be very heady wine, and you can also find yourself ending up one day with nothing. It's important to have other interests. Ronnie always has had them. He also has the basic humility that I think has prevented his character from ever changing.

I hate to sound like a Pollyanna, but I enjoyed my life in Bethesda and Chicago, my college days, Broadway, and Hollywood. I think if I had chosen to continue my career instead of

101

getting married I might have been successful—but the "career" I opted for is the best!

I'm so happy that I arrived in Hollywood in time to get a taste of the Golden Era. Until I met Ronnie, I had no really serious romances in Hollywood, but, of course, I dated. I went to the sneak previews and parties—sometimes at famous actors' homes or in well-known nightclubs. My first date with Ronnie was at Ciro's, a nightclub which is gone now, as is most of that way of life. The Sunset Strip doesn't have the glamour today that it had then, by any means.

Maybe because we all tend to move in circles and choose friends who like to do what we do, we don't see the other side of life. I know I never saw the Hollywood I often heard about—the heavy drinking, pushing starlets in pools, etc. I suppose it existed, but I never saw it.

I do know that in the era of the big studios, Hollywood made more fine films than it does today. Men such as Louis B. Mayer, David O. Selznick, Jack Warner, and Harry Cohn may not have been perfect, but they were giants of the industry and tower above all but a few who operate the business today. They had great power, but for the most part they seemed to use it wisely and well. They were men who censored themselves and so did not need outside censorship.

In the big studio days, these giants brought together many talented people to create movies of quality. Not only producers and directors, actors and actresses, but cameramen, designers, and all the great craftspeople made films that will endure for generations, such as *Gone With the Wind, How Green Was My Valley, Wuthering Heights, Going My Way,* and *The Best Years of Our Lives.*

The contract system developed stars whose brightness will shine forever, such as Gable, Cagney, Tracy, Jimmy Stewart, Bette Davis, Hepburn, Bogart, Gary Cooper, Hank Fonda, John Wayne, and many, many more. They, too, were giants, and I doubt that we will see their likes again because actors today do not get the guidance and the kind of roles on which to build really durable careers.

The giants of yesterday were able to give direction to an industry which today is scattered in a hundred different directions. Hollywood is now in an era of independent filmmakers, who for the most part seem interested only in being more sensational than their rivals. In the Golden Era, Hollywood had the greatest concentration of theatrical skill and talent the world has ever seen.

Although I doubt that the independent system draws as many talented people together as the big studios did, I have no doubt that filmmakers and actors today are as talented as ever, but I think they are being wasted on movies that are more shadow than substance.

To be completely candid, I think most movies nowadays are trash, and many strike me as unhealthy. The explicit sex, pointless violence, and crude language appeal only to our lowest instincts. They have taken away our idealism, our sense of fun and joy. It's chic to be cynical and tear our heroes down. What has happened to us? And what are we doing to our young people?

I'll tell you what I think we've done. We've destroyed our feeling for romance and given young people a distorted picture of what love is. It certainly isn't just sex. Love means giving one's self to another person fully, not just physically. When two people really love each other, this helps them to stay alive and grow. One must really be loved to grow. Love's such a precious and fragile thing that when it comes we have to hold on tightly. And when it comes, we're very lucky because for some it never comes at all. If you have love, you're wealthy in a way that can never be measured. Cherish it.

Movies are a powerful medium. They have great responsibilities which I don't think they're fulfilling. It takes no talent to string together a lot of four-letter words and have people hopping in and out of bed with each other. It does take talent to suggest a relationship, to leave something to the imagination. Now, it's all laid out in front of us to see and it's not a pretty sight. That's just lazy writing.

I believe pointless violence in films is as wrong as explicit sex. There are those who say that the movies are only the mirror of our life today, but movies should show us how to strive to improve the lives we lead, not a degeneration of all we hold high.

At its best, the American way of life is the best way of life, and American movies should reflect this. I think the family has always been the heartbeat and strength of the American way of life. It usually was portrayed with dignity in the past, but is degraded by many current pictures.

There seems to be more violence in society today, but do we have to dwell on it? It's emphasized out of proportion to its reality. I think we're playing a dangerous game by encouraging unbalanced people who see violent acts on film. I deplore the language which is used so freely, and, more often than not, thrown in gratuitously in films. It reminds me of children scribbling on restroom walls.

I cannot accept as admirable a modern morality that makes permissible almost any act. The truly important ingredients of life are still the same as they always have been—true love and real friendship, honesty and faithfulness, sincerity, unselfishness and selflessness, the concept that it is better to give than to receive, to do unto others as you would have them do unto you. These principles are still around, they haven't gone away, but it's not considered chic to discuss them or write about them. I believe these ideals and precepts have endured because they are right and no less right today than yesterday.

I find it interesting that when many of these films are shown on television, they turn out to be better when much of the violence, sex, and language has been cut out. But now there are indications that the television industry is conditioning us to accept sensationalism and vulgarity on that medium, too—possibly because they will soon be running the current crop of movies on daytime TV and The Late Show.

There are shows of the highest quality on television, including, recently, *Roots, The Corn is Green, Backstairs at the White House,* and *Upstairs, Downstairs.* There were sex and violence in some of these but in their proper place, in the proper perspective, and in good taste. Shows such as the Mary Tyler Moore and Carol Burnett Shows have been fine entertainment, in keeping with the tradition of the great musicals and comedies of movies past. There are also programs such as *Sixty Minutes,* which inform us but these are few and far between.

The point is, I think, that I (and, I believe, most of us) would rather be uplifted by a film experience than pulled down by it. I don't deny that life contains the bad as well as the good, and both must be shown in media that depict life as it is, but we are being shown all that is bad and little that is good.

War is violence, but a film such as *Patton* puts it into perspective. General Patton himself was imperfect, but he was a heroic figure and was dealt with heroically in this film. I think we need heroes to emulate in life. In the past, movies did a marvelous job of portraying Pasteur, Zola, Lincoln, Edison; everyone from Madam Curie to Sister Kenny, from Alexander Graham Bell to Sergeant York. Ronnie portrayed George Gipp in the film *Knute Rockne—All American.* It was a movie about football, but the impact that Rockne had on young men went far beyond the football field.

Today, we tear down our heroes. Instead of emphasizing what makes a man more than other men, we look for those shortcomings which show a man to be less than perfect. I prefer to look at the positive side of an FDR, a JFK, a Dwight Eisenhower, a George Custer rather than the negative. I prefer to judge a man by his accomplishments rather than by those faults that merely prove him mortal and as imperfect as any of us.

I will never understand why people feel a need to go on television talk shows to confess private problems. Should we be cynical rather than idealistic? Should we take delight in revealing the flaws in our characters or in the characters of men of accomplishment? Is the exposé more important than the man? Is it better to write a book about the secret life of a hero than to celebrate his successes? Is it better to make a movie about murderers, drug addicts, and prostitutes than about statesmen, artists, and scientists?

For some years now, I haven't liked most of the movies I have seen, and in recent years I have been seeing fewer and fewer of them. I think I am typical of many in the former movie-going public who are turned off by films which are supposed to turn us on.

The filmmakers point to record grosses to support the stands they have taken, but their statistics are deceptive. They charge many times more to see a movie now than they did years ago;

they can make more money now with a far smaller total audience. But they would make much more if they could bring back the audience they have lost. The truth is fewer people are seeing today's pictures; they're just paying more to see them.

Modern filmmakers have lost the majority of their potential customers. And they have not lost them to television but to their own lack of good taste and imagination. Television is not that good; as a matter of fact, a large part of it is mediocre. We are used to it now. We would return to the theaters if there were something good to see.

Moviemakers have lost most of the adult audience. They have insensitively ignored anyone over, say, twenty-five, and seem to appeal primarily to kids looking for kicks. But what is exciting today often is boring by tomorrow. Already I see less nudity and viciousness, hear less ugly language in movie theaters than I did a few years ago. Already these things have become boring. We have seen it all and heard it all by now. In any case, the young people of today will be the adults of tomorrow and less satisfied by sensationalism.

So, which way for the moviemakers to turn? On to new abnormalities? Or back to the old values? I say we should return to films which appeal to the best in us, and to entertainment, to the type of marvelous movies we enjoyed for many years and which I still remember with warmth and pleasure.

Since filmmakers have a great influence on the public, they also owe it to the public to present a true portrayal of life as it is lived and should be lived. American filmmakers have a great responsibility to use their influence wisely because movies have always reflected a view of life in this country that is seen around the world, a depiction of our energy and enthusiasm, pride and presence.

The very people who criticize censorship are inviting it by not censoring themselves.

On the campaign trail, I learned that the average American is dismayed by the movies being made now. They would love to go back to the movies of yesterday and wish they had a say in the way they are made today.

I say they do have such a say. The Joe Smiths of America may be "the little people," but they have strength when they unite. They show their feelings when they stay away from the pictures they don't like but, equally important, patronize the ones they do. This message is bound to reach the moviemakers some day soon. And I hope that among the Joe Smiths there are people of influence in business and industry, men with money who will take it upon themselves to use that influence on the moviemakers and perhaps even become filmmakers themselves.

Let me just add one thing about the stage and screen. As I've said, I enjoyed acting in both, and I feel a sense of loyalty to both. Today's productions are violating a basic theatrical principle—the importance of the audience's imagination.

We've always known that we can portray nothing on stage or screen that will be as effective or dramatic as an audience's imagination. Good theater stimulates our imagination, but today we leave nothing to the imagination. This is particularly true in love scenes which are less romantic than pornographic.

For many years the voluntary Motion Picture Association of America Production Code was an effective system of self-censorship. Yes, the code was restrictive, and sometimes those who worked in pictures thought it was too restrictive. But it made for good writing and exercised the audiences' imagination, which meant good theater.

Here's a classic example from an earlier day. The great director Ernst Lubitsch was doing a picture in which there was a scene of a wedding night. Today there'd be no problem—the audience would witness the wedding night and nothing would be left to the imagination. In that day, however, the production code prevented filming any such thing. A story conference was held and all sorts of proposals were made as to how to fudge on the code, ranging from diaphanous negligees to seductive lighting, etc. Lubitsch listened to all the suggestions and then said, "I won't need the leading man and lady (the bridegroom and bride). Just a hotel corridor." On action, the door to the bridal chamber opened a few inches, a bare feminine arm (belonging to the stand-in) came into view and gently hung a "Do Not Disturb" card on the knob, and the door closed. Each member of the audience could imagine his or her own version of the wedding night with more romance than could be shown on the screen.

No, Hollywood never again will be what it was; none of us will be. But what we all can be is—better.

Chapter 4

Love means many things to many people. As I've said before, for me it means giving more than anything else. It means wanting to give of yourself and your life to another person. And it means sharing, too. If the other person doesn't want to give as you do, then there is something lacking between you. Your own love may be no less, but the feeling between you and the other person is less because it is not shared equally and therefore your life is not shared equally.

I think you know you are in love when *you* no longer are the most important person you know, when there is someone else who is more important to you, when you are more concerned about that person than about yourself. Anything less than that and your life is not all it might be. I would give my life in a minute for my husband and my children, as I would hope they would for me. If you're not sure of this, you're not sure of your love and of being loved. I feel lucky in that I have no doubt of my love and of being loved.

I met my husband in a funny way. Earlier I mentioned that Mervyn LeRoy introduced us. This happened in 1951, during a campaign to clear the film industry of Communist influences. The name "Nancy Davis" had turned up on a list of Communist sympathizers. I have no idea who that Nancy Davis was, but it wasn't me. I knew nothing about politics, nor was I involved in politics. There was no way my friends or family could be considered Communist sympathizers.

As the trade papers gave publicity to these lists, I became very concerned and spoke to my bosses at Metro about it. This was when the columnists Louella Parsons and Hedda Hopper were important in the industry. Louella ran an item stating that the Nancy Davis listed was not me. Actually, I had been receiving announcements of Communist meetings even when I was in New York, and they continued in California.

One day on the set of *East Side, West Side*, I told Mervyn LeRoy how upset I was. Mervyn made my problem his—he is that kind of man. He told me he knew the man who could fix this thing, the president of the Screen Actors Guild, and would speak to him about my problem. And guess who was president of the Screen Actors Guild and a leader in the industry drive against Communists and their sympathizers? Ronald Reagan. Mervyn assured me that Ronnie was a nice young man and I was a nice young woman, and it might be nice if we met. Well, I had seen him in films and, frankly, I had liked what I had seen; so I, too, said I thought that would be very nice.

At home I waited expectantly for the phone to ring. I even checked it a couple of times to make sure it wasn't out of order—it wasn't. It just wasn't being dialed by you-know-who. Well, that's not quite accurate—he was dialing all right, he was calling Mervyn.

On the set the next day, a beaming Mervyn reported that Ronnie Reagan had checked me out, there were at least four Nancy Davises connected with show business, and the Guild would defend my name if it ever became necessary. I told Mervyn that was fine, but I was so worried I'd feel better if the Guild president would call me and explain it all to me. I didn't think that was too much for a constituent to ask of her president. Thank heaven for Mervyn's kindness and his understanding heart. He got the idea. I wanted to meet Ronnie Reagan.

That evening I took up my post by the phone, and this time it rang. Ronnie called to ask if I were free for dinner. I told him it was awfully short notice but I thought I could manage it. He told me it would have to be an early dinner because he had an early call on a film the following morning. I said that was best for me as I, too, had an early call. I didn't, of course, but a girl has to have some pride. He came on crutches. He had broken his leg in a charity baseball game. But he came anyway and took me to LaRue's for dinner. That was one of the popular places on the Sunset Strip when the Strip was still the place to go. To this day, I can still tell you everything we had for dinner, where we sat, and what I wore. My name problem was quickly dismissed because, as Mervyn had already told me, Ronnie had discovered there were other Nancy Davises, so I had no problem. We talked about other things; well, like about a thousand other things.

There were many things that attracted me to Ronnie. He was nice-looking, of course, but he was less like any actor I had ever met in that he did not talk about acting or about the movie he'd made, was making, or was about to make. He had (and has) a very stimulating mind and many interests outside the picture business, and that appealed to me. He's a history buff. He owned a small ranch even then (I knew nothing about horses, but I learned!). He has a marvelous sense of humor and is as great a storyteller as my mother. I loved listening to him—and still do!

Along the way Ronnie discovered that I never had seen Sophie Tucker perform, and she just happened to be opening that night at Ciro's. Despite our "early calls," we decided to hurry over and catch the first show. She was so good, and, since I'd never seen her before, he said maybe we should stay for the second show. We may have stayed for a third; I don't know. I can only tell you it was three in the morning before we got home. We wouldn't have had much sleep before reporting for work—if we'd had to report for work. Of course, neither of us had early calls. He was protecting himself in case I turned out to be a dud. I was protecting my pride.

I don't know if it was love at first sight, but it was something close to it. We were taken with one another and wanted to see more of each other. We had dinner the next night and the night after that and the night after that. We took in all the shows at all the clubs, and there were a lot of clubs in those days. We saw

111

all the Sophie Tuckers I had missed in my life. As soon as we realized that a steady diet of night life wasn't what we really wanted, we started to have quiet evenings, often at the home of Bill and Ardis Holden. Ardis was the movie actress Brenda Marshall. The Holdens were Ronnie's good friends and soon became mine.

Ronnie was born on February 6, 1911, in Tampico, Illinois. His father Jack was an Irish Catholic; his mother Nelle, a Protestant of Scots-English background. His father was a salesman who managed different stores over the years. They moved around Illinois and even lived on the south side of Chicago for a while. That was some years before I lived on the north side. Eventually, they landed in Dixon, ninety miles from Chicago.

Ronnie worked his way through Eureka College, washing dishes in the girls' dormitory (one of his better jobs, he says!) and lifeguarding during the summers. He played football and was captain of the swimming team. Following graduation, he worked as a sports announcer in Iowa and was known as "Dutch" Reagan. The Chicago Cubs used to train at Catalina Island and while he was covering their spring training there in 1937, a friend introduced him to an agent, who took him out to Warner Brothers. The studio gave him a screen test and offered him a contract. He made about fifty films between 1937 and 1964.

At first, he had leading roles, but in what were called B pictures, which were the movies studios made to fill the other half of the double features. Ronnie says for those first couple of years he was the Errol Flynn of the B's.

Then came the kind of break every actor waits for. He was cast as George Gipp ("The Gipper") in the life story of the great football coach Knute Rockne. Pat O'Brien starred in the title role. Ronnie only appeared in one reel; yet it was a perfect part, culminating in the death scene where the Gipper tells Rockne to ask a Notre Dame team if some day they are ever in trouble and up against it to "win one for the Gipper."

This led to what he believes was his greatest role—the part of Drake McHugh in *Kings Row*. When this picture was released in 1942, he achieved instant stardom but by then he was in service in World War II.

One of my favorite pastimes, walking barefoot on the beach.

We had lots of dogs at our Malibu ranch—affectionate, too!

At Malibu we used to breed horses for sale.

Muffin would rather not be photographed.
—PHOTO © ELLEN GRAHAM

Not every cattle ranch has a canoe.
—PHOTO: WALTER ZEBOSKI, AP

Ronnie just before a Western parade—and loving it.

—PHOTO BY GREG A. DALEY

"Those were marvelous, exciting, and interesting years."

—PHOTO BY DENNIS BRACK

One memorable scene in *Kings Row* was the dramatic moment when Drake awakens to discover both his legs have been amputated and, as he struggles, cries out, "Where's the rest of me?" That line became the title of an autobiography Ronnie wrote some years later.

It's funny how the image-making that goes on with people in public life can lead to stereotypes that have no foundation in fact. I'm speaking now of the public life we entered when Ronnie ran for governor. Whenever reference is made to his motion-picture career, it is almost standard practice to say he's an ex-cowboy actor, or that he played in B pictures and was always the nice guy who never got the girl.

Memories can be very short. He left Warner's after thirteen years mainly because they wouldn't put him in western or outdoor pictures, and *Knute Rockne* took him out of the B pictures once and for all. He starred in the film version of some of Broadway's biggest hit shows: *Voice of the Turtle*, *The Hasty Heart*, *John Loves Mary*, to name a few. As for never getting the girl (on the screen, that is), there were Ann Sheridan, Alexis Smith, Eleanor Parker, Patricia Neal, Virginia Mayo, Doris Day, Rhonda Fleming, Barbara Stanwyck, Ginger Rogers, and—well, yes, Nancy Davis on and off screen.

He takes a lot of kidding about a picture called *Bedtime for Bonzo*. He played a professor in this comedy about an experiment having to do with a young chimpanzee. Our good friend Johnny Carson loves to mention this one on his *Tonight Show*. Johnny has a double target for his good-natured kidding because his producer Fred De Cordova directed *Bedtime*. The truth is, it was a very funny and most successful picture.

I think I sensed that acting wasn't completely fulfilling for Ronnie, otherwise he wouldn't have become involved in so many outside activities. He was a six-term president of the Screen Actors Guild, a two-term president of the Motion Picture Industry Council, and was active outside the industry, campaigning for the political candidates of his choice. It took a great deal of time, but he obviously was interested in it and thrived on it. That should have been a clear signal to me so that when our life took the turn it did, I shouldn't have been so surprised. I became a member of the board of the Screen Actors Guild. Contrary to what some people think, it was Ronnie who led me into politics, I didn't lead him.

Ronnie's father had died before we met, but I loved his mother Nelle. She was probably the kindest person (along with my mother) on earth. We always had to hold her down because she would let anyone with a hard-luck story into the house and usually wound up cooking dinner for them. She lived in a house Ronnie had bought for his family near his apartment. His brother Neil and his wife Bess lived a little farther west. Incidentally, there is quite a bit of Nelle in Ronnie. He also likes people and believes in them.

Ronnie and I went together for about a year, but I think I knew from the moment I opened the door on our first date that this was the man for me. Each of us had other dates for awhile, but we soon settled down to just each other. As I got to know him better, I found him to be a strong, warm, sensitive, compassionate man. He is a very sentimental man. How can you resist someone who sends flowers to your mother on your birthday, thanking her for making him the happiest man in the world? We shared the same interests, likes, dislikes. In other words, we were very much alike. Everything fit.

I've often said my life really began with Ronnie, and I think to a great extent it did. What I really wanted out of life was to be a wife to the man I loved and mother to our children. It seemed that everything else had just been a prelude to this.

Soon our friends were taking it for granted we'd marry and we did, too—it was just a matter of when. There was never a really formal proposal as I remember, although Ronnie did call my father and ask him for my hand in marriage—the old-fashioned way. This only endeared him to me more. I used to call my family every Sunday, and I introduced them to Ronnie on the phone. When he'd have to make a trip east, mother would meet him at the train and they'd visit. They soon discovered they both liked to tell stories. It became their practice to save up the latest jokes to tell each other. Needless to say, they became friends immediately. When my father received the request for my hand in marriage, he was delighted to say, "Yes, indeed."

The "when" became more of a problem than we had anticipated. True, in the meantime, I was getting to know his children, Maureen and Mike, by his previous marriage, and they were getting to know me. When we knew we were going to get married, Ronnie sold his small ranch and bought a larger one near Lake Malibu. We'd pile the kids and their friends in the station wagon on Saturdays and head for the ranch, where we'd ride, hike, and have wild games of tag in the pool.

We announced our engagement in February, but then a film came along for Ronnie, so we waited. Then another came along right on the heels of the first, so we waited again. Finally, a third movie came along, and, even though there were just a few days between the two, we decided to get married then and there. Ronnie and Bill Holden were at an Industry Council meeting, and as the agenda dragged on with a lot of routine items, Ronnie finally scribbled on a piece of paper to Bill, "To hell with this, how would you like to be my best man when I marry Nancy?" Aloud, Bill replied, "It's about time." And the two got up and walked out without a word to anyone. I'm sure the others must have wondered what happened to make the Screen Actors Guild representatives walk out.

Once we decided, we moved fast. Since neither of us wanted any publicity or fanfare, we were married at a simple, private ceremony on March 4, 1952, at the Little Brown Church in the Valley, with Ardis and Bill as matron of honor and best man.

I was so excited I went through the ceremony in a daze. The first thing I knew, Bill was saying, "Let me be the first to kiss Mrs. Reagan." I knew you didn't do that in the middle of the ceremony, so I panicked. I motioned madly to him to wait until the ceremony was over. I said, "You're jumping the gun." And he laughed and said, "I am not," and kissed me. I don't even remember Ronnie kissing me. I don't even remember saying our "I do's" or the minister saying he pronounced us man and wife. Ronnie says he did, so I guess we're legal.

I was so out of it I wasn't aware that Bill and Ardis weren't speaking to each other the entire time we were together and actually sat on opposite sides of the church before the ceremony. They had had an argument and, although they were good actors, I think I'd have noticed if I had been thinking straight.

Not only didn't I get a large, formal wedding, as far as I can remember, I didn't get any wedding at all. I do recall getting a piece of wedding cake, which the Holdens had waiting for us at their home in the Toluca Lake area, argument or no argument. And, fortunately, they also had arranged for a photographer to be there, or we wouldn't even have had pictures of our wedding day. As much as I remember of that day, it was fine; I felt just fine about it.

We left the Holdens and drove to Riverside, spending our wedding night in the famous old Riverside Inn. The hotel manager had placed a beautiful bouquet of roses in the bridal suite. The next morning before we left, we delivered them to an elderly woman across the hall we had learned was quite ill. It somehow seemed fitting to share our happiness.

Then we drove to Phoenix and stayed at the Arizona Biltmore on our honeymoon. My parents were vacationing there. They had been alerted to our marriage by phone and were expecting us. Having a honeymoon with your parents may seen strange to some people, but somehow it seemed perfectly natural to us. Perhaps it is a tribute to Ronnie that he took this in stride. Ronnie's mother could not make it to the marriage or the honeymoon. Sadly, she never got to see our son, but before she died she did see our daughter. My parents later retired to Phoenix and the desert life, and live there now.

Because of Ronnie's shooting schedule we had a short honeymoon but a perfect one. The only bad part was driving home and running into a terrible desert wind and sand storm. It started to split the canvas top of his convertible, and the ride home ended with me on my hands and knees on the seat holding the top together so it wouldn't split completely. My hands were frozen, and I thought I would never get out of the kneeling position again. Every once in a while we'd have to stop so I could stretch and rub some warmth back into my hands. As you can imagine, I tease Ronnie fairly often about this "perfect" end to a perfect honeymoon.

After we returned, Ronnie resigned as president of the Screen Actors Guild, though he did return later to serve a sixth and final term as president when he was asked to help negotiate a new contract with the producers. He was active in industry politics for as long as he was active in Hollywood, and there's no doubt this hurt his acting career. When producers are casting pictures, they envision various actors in the roles. When they have spent years at the negotiating table across from an actor or served on industry committees with him, this can influence how they think of him. It's difficult for them to visualize him leading a calvary charge or heading off the rustlers at Eagle Pass. When Ronnie was trying to talk his way into a Western, he once told Jack Warner that if Jack ever did give him a Western he would probably cast him as the lawyer from the east.

Ronnie needed a lot of moral support when we first were married. His finest film *Kings Row* made him a star while he was in the service, and for more than four years he was unable to follow up on it. Returning from the Army Air Force, he found himself all but forgotten. He traded Warner Brothers three films for the remaining three years of his contract and began to freelance. He was offered a lot of films but few good ones. He had made a lot of bad movies in the early part of his career when he was just starting, and he didn't want to go back to making that kind of film again. We talked it over and decided to wait for better opportunities. Waiting it out without working was hard on the budget, but we got by.

Then in 1954, Ronnie was given an opportunity to represent General Electric and host the weekly *General Electric Theater* program on television. He was to star in four shows a year and introduce the program each week. The contract also called for him to go on the road a total of ten weeks a year, meeting GE employees and speaking to various groups at luncheons and banquets. Soon he was not only speaking to GE employees and touring plants all across the country, but also appearing at Chambers of Commerce, United Fund Drives, and, at the end, national conventions. All this experience would prove to be invaluable in preparing him for the sort of life that lay ahead of us, but we had no idea of that at the time. He was away from home a little too much to satisfy either of us. In the eight years the show lasted, he visited 139 GE plants in 38 states. Then he hosted *Death Valley Days* on television for two years. When he left to enter politics, our good friend (and godfather to our son) Bob Taylor took over as host.

When Ronnie and I returned from our honeymoon, we moved into my apartment. But it was tiny, so Ronnie kept his apartment, too, as a place to keep his possessions and a lot of his clothes while we hunted for a house. We sort of divided our life between the two apartments. There were times when we were going out and he'd have to go to his apartment to dress. We ate out most of the time, but this was all right because I can't cook very well.

I remember once when I was alone with my father and wanted to make coffee. I put the pot on the stove and couldn't understand why nothing happened. He patiently pointed out that even on a gas stove you can't expect anything to heat up on the pilot light alone. We all have our talents but cooking isn't one of mine. I know I said I wanted to be a wife and a mother; I never said I wanted to be a cook. I love everything that goes with "homemaking." I read recipe books by the hour, and I'm sure I'm a frustrated interior decorator.

We found a nice little house that I really loved in the hills of the Pacific Palisades. This area is in the far western part of Los Angeles, near the ocean, a little bit off the beaten track. A lot of our friends felt we were foolish to move so far from the heart of Hollywood, but we wanted to be farther out of town and have never regretted it. Our first child, our daughter Patti, was born while we were living in this house. Ronnie had an olive tree planted for me as a surprise for my return from the hospital. I still see it when I drive by this house and feel a little tug at my heart.

About four years later in 1956, we felt we needed a larger house and built one nearby in these hills, where we have lived all but a few months of our marriage.

It is a three-bedroom house, not really large but large enough. There are other houses all around us, but each is set apart a little. We are surrounded by the Santa Monica Mountains and greenery, and on a clear day we really can see Catalina Island. We have our privacy. We have lived here more than twenty years now, and we have to repair the place a bit, but it's worth it. It's a lovely house, a lovely area, and I don't think we'd ever leave it. We had to live in another house in Sacramento while Ronnie was governor, of course, but we never considered giving up our home. Our second child, our son Ron, was born while we were living here.

We had to sell our ranch at Lake Malibu when Ronnie became governor, and that wasn't easy to do for we loved it dearly. All of the children's birthday parties had taken place there, and I can still see myself pushing some young one on the swing we had hung from a tree in the yard. It's a family joke that Ronnie married me just to get someone to paint the fences. We put a lot of ourselves into that place. But Ronnie had taken a large cut in income when he left television to become governor. We simply could not afford the luxury of a ranch.

We always knew of course that once our years in Sacramento ended, we'd want another ranch, so off and on we'd go ranch hunting. The one at Lake Malibu had spoiled us. It was only a thirty-five-minute drive from our home in the Palisades, and yet it was completely country. We could drive up there and spend the day in the wooded hills, where it was possible even to come upon a mountain lion. Deer also roamed the place, and yet we could be back in town for dinner.

We soon found out there was no ranch available within a half hour of our home; the real-estate boom had taken care of that. Two of our closest friends, Betty and Bill Wilson, knew of our dream and knew the kind of place we were looking for—less a farm than a chunk of wilderness.

One weekend when we were at their ranch north of Santa Barbara, Bill said he had something he thought we should see. The four of us piled in his car and started up a narrow mountain road, paved with asphalt but very narrow. It would be wrong to call it a winding road; it was just a plain switchback trail. We were only on it for seven miles, but it seemed to me like seventy. Betty urged him to turn around saying there couldn't possibly be a ranch where we were going. I must confess I thought she was right, but I figured Ronnie could speak up if he wanted to. I'd keep quiet.

Bill turned off the road and through a gate. We wound along a gravel lane, through a forest of live oaks, and suddenly we were looking down across a sloping meadow toward a cluster of farm buildings. I didn't know it then but we had found our ranch. It overlooks the ocean on one side and the Santa Ynez Valley on the other from a saddle ridge 2,400 feet up in the Santa Ynez Mountains.

When he got out of the car and met the owner Ray Cornelius (a cattleman) and his wife, I took a quick look at Ronnie and knew he'd already decided—this was it. The Corneliuses were wonderful people and very sympathetic with our problems of having to care for the place on a catch-as-catch-can basis whenever we could get away from Sacramento. We took possession several weeks before Ronnie's second term as governor ended.

The Corneliuses had a home down the mountain and therefore did not live at the ranch. The main house was a small ninety-year-old adobe which they used about as much as we had used our Malibu ranch since they also could be home in half an hour. For us it would be a two-and-a-half-hour drive. So we'd go there when we could stay for a few days, which meant we'd need to do some work on the house.

It's funny when you start on a project how your original plans expand. We set out to do some interior painting and wound up knocking out a wall, tiling the floors, putting on a tile roof to add to the Mexican flavor of the house, and adding a stone patio. And when I say "we," I mean "we."

In the first few weeks Ronnie was still governor. We'd come down from Sacramento for a weekend, making the round trip each day, five hours of driving for about five hours' work. The security detail who had been with us during those eight years would pitch in as if it were their house, too. We never asked them to, that wasn't their job, they just did it. It was proof of something we're very proud of; they had become our friends. It was a sad day when we parted company.

But the work went on. Now our work force was only ourselves, Lee Clearwater, who had become our ranch foreman, and "Barney" Barnett, who had been assigned to the governor by the highway patrol until his retirement. When Barney retired, he stayed on as an aide and friend.

Lee took charge of putting in the large lawn we wanted, the

orchard, and vegetable garden. We and Barney took care of the house, patio, stables, and corrals. Ronnie had installed a white, Kentucky-type post-and-rail fence at the Malibu ranch—about two miles of it—but he didn't consider it suitable for either our adobe house or the wild beauty of our new ranch. He drew different types of fence to scale on drafting paper before finally settling on one made from telephone poles.

He and Barney took about 120 poles and sawed the bottom six feet from each one to set in the ground as posts. Then they cut fifteen-foot lengths from the remainder of the poles, notched the ends, and cut notches in the posts with a chain saw, chisel, and hammer. The poles were fitted in the posts, and now we have a solid, rustic-looking fence that goes with our adobe house.

We haven't stopped working yet. Someone asked when we thought the place would be finished, and we said we hoped never. It's fun for me to take something and try and fix it up. I wasn't able to help put in a telephone-pole fence, but I kept busy inside the house while that was going on.

Our only heating system is fireplaces, so there is always wood to cut. When we aren't doing some specific chore, we cut brush and prune trees in the groves of oak and madrone trees.

I think it's important to have a place where you can be by yourself and recharge your batteries. At our place we truly do look to the hills from whence cometh our strength.

When you lead a public life, it's especially important to have a private place. And when you've done all the work yourself, that place becomes all the more precious to you.

Ronnie built a pier into a little lake on the property. Sometimes we take out the canoe *Truluv*, which Ronnie had given me. The flowers and vegetables are flourishing. The young fruit trees have not yet begun to bear fruit, but will be beautiful when they do.

The ranch is for Ronnie, but I enjoy it as much as he does; maybe more so because it's a place I can get him alone and away for a weekend from time to time, or over a holiday. We really love ranch life.

We run cattle through the grazing season and sell them off for the increase in weight, then buy a new herd of grazers for the new season. At our Malibu ranch we used to breed horses for sale. They were racing thoroughbreds and were sold at the yearling sales. Now our horses are for riding and cattle herding.

The kids sometimes ride, but they rode a lot more when they really were kids. Patti rides well and likes it a lot. I ride now and enjoy it. Ronnie loves riding and is great. He even jumps, whereas I ride around the jumps!

I remember the first time he got me up on a horse, he told me to take charge. I was sitting so high up I didn't think I could reach the ground if I jumped. It reminded me of a *New Yorker* magazine cartoon which showed a tiny little lady sitting high atop this enormous horse with the man down below telling her to show the horse who was boss. That first time I was that tiny little lady, and the horse and I both knew who was the boss. But all that has changed. There is no way to describe the beauty of riding trails flanked in the spring by buckthorn and wild lilac in bloom and so fragrant you can hardly bear it. There are spots on the ranch from which you can see the ocean, the channel islands on one side and the whole Santa Ynez Valley spread out on the other. Ronnie had always told me that everything looked different from the back of a horse, and he was right.

The first horse Ronnie owned was a black thoroughbred mare named Baby which he rode in the picture *Stallion Road.* He bought her before they finished filming. Later he rode her again in *The Last Outpost,* in which he played a Confederate cavalry officer. He is now riding her son Little Man. Baby was retired and died while we still owned the Malibu ranch.

In addition to the horses, we've had lots of dogs and cats at the ranch. We've taken in strays and some that were abandoned by their owners. I remember one of our dogs had pups when we moved to Sacramento. When they were six weeks old and weaned, we had them driven to Sacramento to be with us. When they got out of the car after being cooped up for about eight hours, the pups ran free, right into a swimming pool out back. Fully dressed, I jumped in to save them. It was wintertime, cold and damp. We had just moved into the house, and I had assumed the pool was heated. I soon found out this one wasn't! I don't know if the pups could swim, but I fished them out.

We keep two dogs at our home in the Palisades. One is called Lady, a Belgian Shepherd who had been thrown out of a car on the freeway. She was found, brought to us, and we took her in. She must have been mistreated by the man who owned her. She distrusts men, except for Ronnie, but she is fine with women. The other dog, Muffin, is a Cockapoo (a cross between a Cocker Spaniel and a Poodle), who was given to me by a friend. The two make quite a combination. Lady barks like crazy at every car and person coming up our circular driveway, and Muffin joins in. They make a real racket, but they are good watchdogs and dear pets. No one can come up the driveway without my knowing well in advance.

I have been very happy with my homes, but homes really are no more than the people who live in them.

Chapter 5

When I was married, I immediately wanted to have children. I was close to thirty years old and didn't want to wait. Ronnie was just past forty, and he wanted us to have children, too. I became pregnant early in our marriage and really looked forward to our first child.

When Patti was born, we certainly broke the old tradition of the frantic father and the calm, well-prepared mother. In the first place she wasn't due for about another four or five weeks. We were at a horse show in the old Pan Pacific Auditorium, sitting in a box with some friends. Their daughter had borrowed one of our mares, Mrs. Simpson, to ride in a class for open jumpers. We'd named her Mrs. Simpson because she was the only horse we owned that wasn't an English thoroughbred. She was pure American—a quarter horse.

Early in the show I thought the baby was changing positions and whispered it to Ronnie. A little later the same thing happened, and again I kept him informed. When it happened a third time, he told me to squeeze his arm every time it happened. Just before the show ended, he whispered, "Say good-bye to your friends fast, you're having a baby." I said, "That's ridiculous." After all, I was a doctor's daughter, and a doctor had told me the baby wasn't due for several more weeks. I told Ronnie it must be cramps. He said, "Well, you're having those cramps every eighteen minutes." He'd been timing me every time I squeezed his arm.

I told him, "That's crazy." "We'd better go to the hospital" was his reply. But I said, "No, let's go home," and I made the poor man drive me all the way home to the Palisades. At the horse show we were only twenty minutes from the hospital; at home we were an hour away. But home we went, got undressed, and went to bed. Then the contractions started coming harder and faster, and I decided he had been right all along. We dressed and drove all the way back across town to Cedars of Lebanon Hospital, having called our doctor, Benbow Thompson, who met us there. We were sent to a labor room, and Ronnie kept on timing the contractions. He said, "I think they've forgotten us." With my faith in the profession, I assured him they knew what they were doing and would come for me when it was time. Finally, he went to the door, stopped a passing nurse, and told her the contractions were coming every ninety seconds. He had been right again. He was almost trampled in the rush to get me to the delivery room.

Then the long wait began. For some reason, the baby just didn't come. Hours passed. Ronnie still talks about the fact that the couch in the waiting room had a big hole in it and was broken right down the middle. He just couldn't get comfortable. Other fathers were waiting, of course, but their babies would arrive and they would leave. Fathers would come in with their hands full of coins and make all the calls fathers usually make to family and friends after a baby is born, while Ronnie waited. Fourteen hours passed. The night turned into day. Then Dr. Thompson came and told Ronnie that he didn't think they should wait any longer, that it wasn't good for me and wasn't good for the baby, and they wanted permission to perform a Cesarean section. Ronnie gave his permission to go ahead, but it only increased his anxiety.

Although fourteen hours certainly was a long wait, they had obviously sedated me because I don't recall having any pain. I do remember being so woozy in the delivery room that I started to introduce the different doctors and nurses to each other because I thought maybe they weren't acquainted. They assured me they

134

did know one another. Later they laughed about it and told me I had acted like a hostess at a dinner party.

None of the forms of natural childbirth were popular at that time and Ronnie wasn't able to be in the delivery room with either of our babies as so many fathers are these days. In fact, when I was back in my room and the nurses brought me our baby for the first time, my first thought was that it was sad that Ronnie couldn't be there because this was a moment meant to be shared by father and mother. We named her Patricia Ann, though we've always called her Patti. I finally had the baby I had wanted for so long.

My second thought was that she sure had a lot of hair for a baby. And then I thought that Ronnie might be disappointed he had a daughter instead of a son. For some reason, I had been sure I was going to have a boy. I needn't have worried. Ronnie told my mother that having a daughter would be like seeing me as a little girl in all the years before he knew me. When Mother told me this I started to cry, then she started to cry, and we had a grand time together.

Above all, we were happy that she was healthy. One thing I hadn't expected was how difficult it had turned out for me to deliver and, as a consequence, the element of risk in the birth. We were subsequently told that once a mother delivers by Cesarean section, all other births must be this way. And while we wanted to have another child soon, it was close to six years before we could. I had a couple of miscarriages during that time.

When I became pregnant with our second child Ron, Dr. Thompson, who was due to retire, told me he would stay on for the birth if I agreed to stay in bed for three months, have hormone shots weekly, and take it easy all the way. I agreed because I had a lot of faith in him. He'd seen me through my first delivery, and I wanted him to see me through my second. He was a dear man who, sadly, died just a few years later.

Doctor Thompson couldn't have taken better care of me. It was difficult lying in bed for three months. And it was hard to be very careful with every movement I made the rest of the time. But it was also difficult keeping the baby, and every time I moved I thought I might lose him.

135

You don't wait to go into labor when you are going to have a Cesarean delivery, so I went to the hospital when Dr. Thompson told me it was time, and the delivery was much easier and much faster than my first. But, of course, carrying this baby had been much harder and more worrisome. Still, he caused no problem in the delivery, even though he was big and healthy.

When on May 20, 1958, the nurse held up our baby for me in the delivery room and Benbow said, "Look, Nancy, you got your wish—it's a boy," I wanted to say something like "Whoopee," but I was so groggy I couldn't get it out. But I was the happiest girl in town. My world seemed so complete—little did I know it was gradually beginning to change and I would enter another new stage.

We named our son Ronald Prescott Reagan, so he is not technically a Junior to his papa Ronald Wilson Reagan. I have called him Ron at times in this book so as not to confuse readers. Ronnie nicknamed him "Skipper" early on. We called him that for many years, and I may find myself calling him that when I am talking about him as a boy. But from about the time he entered high school, he decided Skipper was too boyish a name and asked us to call him Ron. So, Ron it is.

Just as Maureen and Michael have some of the characteristics of their mother or father, so do Patti and Ron. Each is distinctly different from the others. Patti is tall and like Ronnie in build. She has my coloring and dark eyes, but her eyes are shaped like Ronnie's. Ron has my coloring and dark eyes, but his eyes are shaped like mine.

Michael and his wife, the former Colleen Sterns, presented Ronnie with his first grandchild, Cameron Michael, on May 30, 1978. We both dote on him but don't get to see him as much as we'd like. Mike and Colleen live in the San Fernando Valley. Mike used to race boats and now sells them. Maureen, who was married but isn't at present, did very well with a radio talk show for a while and is busy now with an acting career.

Our two younger children definitely are different in personality, although both are artistic in nature. They both write and paint well. Patti is interested in singing and acting and Ron in dancing and writing. I think you have to let your children find their own paths and their own lives. I believe parents make a mistake if they try to force their children into what they think they should do.

Both Patti and Ron had most of their schooling here in Los Angeles. When it was time for Patti to start high school, she went to the Orme School, a private coeducational school in Arizona. She had gone to summer camp there, loved the western life, horseback riding, and the school, and Orme was close to my parents' home in Phoenix.

When Ronnie became governor, Ron transferred from a school in Los Angeles to one in Sacramento. But when it was time for him to start high school, Ronnie was in the middle of his second term. So Ron returned to Los Angeles and went to the Webb School, a private boys' boarding school. He would only have to be there for two years, and came home once a month for a long weekend. He didn't want to face changing high schools in the middle; we talked it over and decided this would be best. Yet when we returned, he transferred to Harvard School in Los Angeles and finished there because he didn't want to go on boarding out. He preferred to live at home, and that certainly was fine with us.

Prior to politics, we were luckier than most families because Ronnie's work periods came in specified chunks of time, leaving long stretches of free time in between. Therefore, we had more hours to spend together as a family than most. I didn't realize how spoiled I'd been until we made the change. If you could pick the ideal time to go into politics, it would be when the children are grown and settled because there's no doubt that political life is difficult for them. I think Patti was the least happy about her father's new career, but I think she realizes now he's doing what he wants to do and what he feels is important.

Ron had it harder in many ways because he had to make more adjustments. Patti stayed in the same school, while Ron, as the son of the governor, had to change schools and move to Sacramento when he was eight years old. I made a rule that I had to be home by four when Ron got back from school. I tried to make his life as normal as possible, though I'm sure it gave me a few gray hairs and didn't always please the security people. Ron went to school in a car pool and bicycled around the neighborhood like everyone else. But children can be cruel, as we all know. I can remember going out to watch him play football on his fifth-grade team and hearing players on the other team say, "There's Reagan —let's get him." He never mentioned it to me, but I practically had to be held back from going after those boys. Mothers are the same the world over, I guess, but it's hard to hear such things and do nothing. Hard? It really tears you apart inside.

While it may look from the outside as if we never led a normal life, it always was as normal as we could make it and always seemed normal to us. Just as I was raised with theater and screen stars as family friends, so were our children. Aside from Bill and Ardis Holden, Bob and Ursula Taylor were extremely close friends. Dick and June Powell and Edgar and Frances Bergen were also dear friends, as was Jimmy Cagney. There have been many, and they mean much to me.

Bill and Ardis and Colleen Moore were Patti's godparents, and Bob and Ursula Taylor were Ron's. We are the godparents to the Taylors' daughter Tessa, who is a joy. I think Bob's death hit me as hard as anything in my life. He smoked too much and had a wracking cough that worried us all. We tried to get him to see a doctor about it but he wouldn't. Now we think he suspected what was really wrong. When he finally did give in, the end came much too soon. Bob Taylor was a wonderful man, and we still feel his loss deeply. I spent as much time as I could at the hospital with Ursula and him—everyone knowing it was just a matter of time but no one saying it.

The last time I saw him, I left the hospital to go back to Sacramento, telling Ursula I'd see her in a few days. I got out in the hall, and something made me turn back. I returned to his room and kissed him on the cheek. When I landed in Sacramento, they told me he had died. They had tried to stop the plane but couldn't. I flew back on the next plane to be with Ursula. She asked if Ronnie would deliver the eulogy and, of course, he said yes. But the morning of the funeral he confessed to me that he was afraid he wouldn't be able to get through it without breaking up. I wasn't sure he would either. We were both right. He was able to get out about two sentences, then his voice broke and he was fighting back the tears. He managed to finish, but with great difficulty. We have a tape of the eulogy but have never played it to this day—I'm not sure when it'll ever be possible for us to listen to it. I know it was typically Ronnie, tender and warm and with some humor. Just what Bob would have wanted, I'm sure.

During one of the last conversations I had with Bob in the hospital, he said to me, "Help Ursula to find a nice man. Just a nice man." As it worked out, I didn't have to help her. A nice man found her, and in due time they were married. She's a beautiful woman, inside as well as out, and we are very happy for her.

It's wonderful to add new friends to your life, but even more so to hold on to the old ones you've had for years. At this stage of my life I don't have the chance to build up new thirty-year friendships, so I cherish the ones I have! Because of the twist our lives took, we can't be with our friends as often as we'd like, but we're always in touch with them. They've been with us during some very important moments in our lives. I certainly don't know what I'd have done without my friends at the conventions, for instance, and I'm terribly sentimental about them. But then, I'm terribly sentimental, period. Ronnie says I can cry sending out the laundry!

I have mentioned that our political life was difficult for the children, and I believe it was and is. But sometimes when I hear children of well-known people blaming all their problems on their parents' prominence—whether it's in politics or movies or whatever—I pull back just a little and wonder whether maybe they're not copping out a bit. I've seen some children from that background do very well for themselves.

These are difficult times to be teenagers—they're exposed to so many more things than they were years ago. Certainly when I went to school, there were no drug pushers in the school playgrounds. You weren't bombarded with as much violence or sexual permissiveness as you are now. But it's also a difficult time to be a parent. If only young people could realize how very much their parents want to insure happiness for them and how deep their parents' heartaches can be. Parents aren't always right, but they try to be right and can only go by experience. I believe strongly in the family unit, and I'm disturbed by what seems to me to be a gradual erosion of it. I think the family is the root of our country's strength, and its downgrading—whether it is intentional or not—is both frightening and dangerous.

For a long time I've thought about the absence of courage, the decline of standards, the loss of values, and the disappearance of quality that seem to be afflicting our country. I believe in the "indoctrination," if you will, of moral values. As Leo Rosten remarked in an interview with Eric Severeid, "I believe you have a debt to those who have taken care of you, that you have a duty to whatever it is God or Fate gave you—to use the mind, brain and heart, not to whine so much and not to blame society for every grievance."

When Alexander Solzhenitsyn won the Nobel Prize, he said, "One word of truth shall outweigh the whole world." One word of truth which remains constant despite efforts to erase it from the language is morality—and I mean it in the broadest sense, not just sexual morality. Morality is a word whose meaning can provide us an anchor in the worst storms and one I believe we should try to instill in our children. We may fail in our attempt but at least we should try. We should always try.

Human beings need moral standards to guide them. Society needs them to keep it from flying apart. Moral standards evolve, of course. They're not fixed in the stars. We need such standards because they encourage the most important asset of civilized people—self-restraint. Self-restraint marks the difference between adult and childish behavior. A grown person who lives without self-control can have no central purpose in his or her life.

Each generation challenges the mores of the last one. We did it. Our children are doing it. And so will their children. But it's a mistake for any generation to just toss aside the lessons of history simply because they're old. The philosopher George Santayana once wrote, "Those who cannot remember the past are condemned to repeat it." He was right. Most of what is sometimes referred to as old-fashioned has endured because it's basically right.

I keep hearing about the "new morality," but I don't really think it's all that new. It may be as old as Babylon or the final days of the Roman Empire. I suspect it may very well be a retreat from involvement, from all the risks that go along with getting one's feelings wrapped up in commitments to others. That, of course, is what marriage is all about. It's filled with risks, with the likelihood of sorrow and the hope of joy and, ultimately, the promise of deep human fulfillment, but with no money-back guarantees.

I believe in marriage and the marriage contract, and I couldn't live any other way. I believe in standing up and committing yourself before God, the law, and your family and friends to another person and a way of life. Anything less is playing house. I've always wanted to belong to somebody and to love someone who belonged to me. I always wanted someone to take care of me, someone I could take care of.

That doesn't mean that I don't believe in an independence of mind and spirit because I do. Ronnie and I don't agree on everything. There's no one on earth you agree with all the time. But we talk things over, express our opinions, listen to one another, and learn from each other. I have my own interests and causes in which I'm interested. I think it's very important for a woman to have them. Indeed, I think it's essential.

Marriage certainly isn't easy, and it takes a lot of effort to make it work. Whoever said it was fifty-fifty was crazy. Many times it's ninety-ten or seventy-five-twenty-five, but you have to be willing to bend a little when it's necessary. Somehow I get the feeling that many people don't work at marriage as much as they used to, or bend when they should. In today's climate it's easier to walk away when something goes wrong—and I feel sorry for those who do. If they only knew that those problems—the ups and downs that you work out and somehow survive—often make a marriage stronger. I realize I've been lucky. I remember Mervyn LeRoy in my prayers every night! I certainly can't imagine life without Ronnie and don't ask me where the last twenty-seven years have gone!

I'm against abortion unless the mother's life is in danger. I've never been able to get past the idea that you're taking a life. Patti had a teacher in school who said to her class, "Suppose a pregnant woman had a window in her tummy through which she

141

could see her baby grow and take it out and hold it. At what point do you think she'd decide it was all right to kill it?" Which is a pretty graphic way of saying what I'm trying to say.

Ronnie used to have high school students come to the governor's office every week. These visits were shown on a taped closed-circuit TV program for use in the schools that was sponsored by the State Department of Education. The programs were unrehearsed, and Ronnie had no idea in advance what the questions would be. One day, the students got on the subject of abortion and asked if that wasn't better than having an unwanted child grow up unloved and possibly become a criminal. Ronnie told them how many childless couples there were just waiting to adopt unwanted babies. Usually, when the taping was over, the students would hang around and ask a few more questions. This particular day a girl, who hadn't asked any questions during the program, shyly raised her hand. She said, "Governor, I'm adopted. I think a great deal of my parents and they think a lot of me." Then she paused and added, "I'm glad someone didn't kill me." When he came home that evening, Ronnie said, "If only she'd said that when the cameras were on so all those others could have heard."

To make matters worse, we find our welfare programs making abortions available to underage girls regardless of their family's financial situation, even without informing the family. It seems to me this is government interference in family relationships at the highest level. A letter from one mother really said it all for me. She wrote,

> Who do they think they are—not telling the parents? Who in God's name gave them the right to keep the health and welfare of your own child from you? I, as a mother, have the right to carry in my body my unborn child. I have a right to stay up night after night holding and pacing the floor with this child, feeling the pain of fear. I have a right to look into her tiny face and love her so much that I could squeeze her to death. I have a right to watch her grow day after day, year after year. And then one day to look up and see a 15-year-old young lady standing in front of me. A 15-year-old who might someday find herself in terrible trouble

142

and some fool is standing there saying I don't have a right to know. I repeat—who do they think they are?

Children need love, understanding, patience, guidance, discipline. We all know this, but these qualities can't be dispensed by the government or the schools or television sets. These can never take the place of parents. I'm sure we've all had some disappointments, large or small, from some of the choices our children have made as they were growing up. Willa Cather wrote, "There are only two or three human stories and they go on repeating themselves as fiercely as if they had never happened before." If only we could convince our children we've passed through all those stages, too, and really do understand their problems.

I certainly don't mean to give the impression that I have a magic formula for raising children to be "good people." I don't. But in all the question-and-answer sessions I've experienced, it was easy to learn this is the one area—the family—that's of deep concern to people everywhere. Isn't it strange that the most important task we perform in life—being a parent—we have absolutely no training for? The parent-child relationship may be the most intimate and enduring of all. People can walk away from the man-woman relationship a lot easier.

Ronnie and I go to the Bel-Air Presbyterian Church, where the minister is Donn Moomaw, a former football star at UCLA. Donn is a tall, good-looking man and a speaker you really look forward to hearing. His church is filled every Sunday, and a large number of the people who attend are young. I think it's easy for young people to identify with Donn, and it is marvelous to see. He has played an important part in our lives on a number of occasions. I feel very close to him. We both have faith in God and believe He has a plan for each of us.

When people ask me, "But what can I do? I'm only one person," I always remind them, "It was one woman who took prayer out of the school." No one can convince me that this was the wish of the majority of the people. I believe, in spite of her action, that God really is right there in the schoolroom, as He is everywhere. I think that in today's world, people are hungry for something to believe in and He's there waiting for them. I believe that we need God in our lives and that it's possible for one person to put Him back into our schoolrooms and families.

Ronnie lives with this sense of duty in him that takes him away from his family a great deal, so I've had to do a lot of the rearing and disciplining of the children. Like many parents, most of our disagreements have been about how to deal with the children and their problems. I've always hesitated to pile the problems of a child or two on top of him when he's just returned home from dealing with the problems of millions of people. However, when one of our children has asked for his help, he or she has always gotten it.

I remember one time his eldest son Mike was going through a difficult time and turned to Ronnie for comfort and counsel. Ronnie took all the time his son needed and gave him all the help he could. Later, Mike told an interviewer how much it had meant to him. If the parent-child relationship has developed to the point where respect continues throughout life, you've achieved a great deal.

I'm sure my children don't agree with all my beliefs—or their father's. I don't think I was a perfect parent (and they weren't perfect children), but I did my best. That's all I ask of them. There comes a time when you have to let them go and hope they take with them things of value you have tried to give them. I love my two children, as well as the two I inherited by marriage.

I'm equally sure that not everyone who reads this book will agree with everything I've written, but I've said it in all the interviews and all the question-and-answer sessions when asked, so I might as well say it here. But if you feel as I do, don't give up. The main things I discovered during Ronnie's campaigns is that there are millions of people around the country who feel as I do. Take heart.

—PHOTO BY C. LYDON LIPPINCOTT

Ronnie campaigned for Barry Goldwater in 1964. Duke Wayne helped Ronnie when he ran for Governor in 1966 and 1970.

An interesting double exposure of our midnight inauguration.

For a technical reason Ronnie was sworn in twice as Governor. Our son Ron (above) was obviously intrigued.

At the concert the night before the Inaugural Ball.

Ronnie speaking at the Inaugural Ball.

The governor's mansion (above) from which we had to move. The house (below) we moved into was in a quiet residential neighborhood. We lived there for the rest of the time in Sacramento.

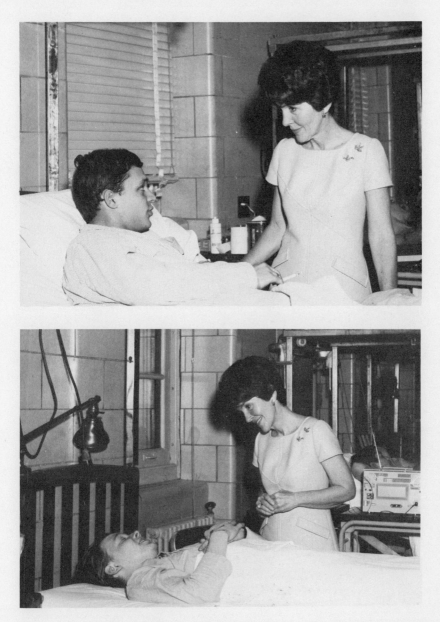

In February 1969 I visited wounded veterans at the National Naval
Medical Center, Bethesda, Maryland.

Visits to Shannon Clancy and Patrick Moore at the Children's Hospital
Medical Center, Oakland, 1970.

Chapter 6

If I never imagined myself the wife of a political leader, I certainly never pictured myself on the campaign trail. Yet it has been one of the most interesting, revealing, and rewarding experiences I've ever had. Yes, it's tiring, but I wouldn't have traded it for anything.

Looking back on it, it seems as if I should have been able to see it coming. In one of our scrapbooks there's a clip from a movie-magazine story on Ronnie which reads, "If Ronald Reagan wasn't an actor, he would more than likely be the president of a big bank in the town in which he lived, or the mayor, or a senator, or something important." Within the movie industry, he always did much more than act. All of his activities as president of the Screen Actors Guild and chairman of the Motion Picture Industry Council were to serve him in good stead later when he entered politics. Right after World War II, when the Communists tried to gain control of the motion-picture industry through subversion and infiltration of several Hollywood unions, Ronnie, as president of the Guild, found himself in the forefront of the battle. A well-known actor who had gone along with the Communists for awhile and then became disillusioned was asked what had stopped the Communists from taking over the industry. He replied, "We ran into a one-man battalion named Ronald Reagan."

* * *

In guiding the Screen Actors Guild through the six-month strike of 1959, Ronnie did more for the bit players than for the stars and, in the end, secured a pension and health-care plan for Guild members. Over some twenty years of negotiating the basic contract between the actors and the producers, he learned a great deal about the art of negotiation. The insights into big business that he gained while representing General Electric over eight years were considerable.

We didn't know it but he was being drawn deep into the political waters. And yet he never considered running for public office, believing his contribution would be to campaign for those who did. He had grown up a Democrat and, at one time in those postwar years, he had been asked to run for Congress. He refused to even consider it.

But something was happening that he wasn't aware of or possibly couldn't admit to himself. His public speaking during those years with General Electric had made him something of a national figure and very much in demand as a speaker. He had always done his own research and speeches and, while at first the speeches dealt with the problems of the motion-picture industry, they gradually began to be concerned with free enterprise in general and government's encroachment on the marketplace. One day he came home from a speaking trip and told me he was beginning to realize that the people he had campaigned for in election years—the Democrats—were responsible for the things he was speaking out against between elections.

In watching him, I discovered that changing party affiliation could be as difficult and emotional an experience as changing one's religion. In 1960 he helped campaign for the Republican ticket but as a Democrat. By this time he knew he could no longer follow the Democratic leadership. As he tells it, the party had left him, he didn't leave the party. It no longer stood for the ideas and principles that had drawn him to it as a young man. Winston Churchill, who also changed political parties, said it best: "Some men change principle for party and some men change party for principle."

When the 1962 campaign came along in California, Ronnie was out on the speaking circuit as a Republican and yet he still hadn't re-registered. He was speaking at a banquet one night when a woman in the audience interrupted to ask if he'd re-registered. He said no. She said, "Well, I'm a registrar," and marched up to the podium. He signed up and then continued his speech to a very enthusiastic audience.

Now it was the Republicans' turn to ask him to be a candidate —twice for the United States Senate and once for the governorship. Again he declined, saying, "Pick the candidate and I'll campaign for him." Which he did.

In 1964 he became the state cochairman of the Citizens for Goldwater Committee and spoke all over California in Barry's behalf. A group of prominent Republicans asked him if he would speak on national television if they raised the money to buy the time. We didn't know it at the time but that TV speech would change our lives. We've been told that the party received more than $8 million in contributions as a result of that one television appearance.

The Republican party had been badly split by the bitterness of the 1964 primaries, and nowhere was it more divided than in California. In 1965 a group of Republican leaders, including several of our close personal friends, came to the house one evening. They wasted no time in stating their mission. They wanted Ronnie to enter the 1966 governor's race against the Democratic incumbent, who was seeking a third term. They put their request on the basis that Ronnie was the only one who could reunite the party and win the election.

Again Ronnie told them to find a candidate and he'd campaign for him. He explained there was no way that we could afford to turn our lives upside down and walk away from a career that he'd been in for almost thirty years. We went to bed that night, certain that the issue was settled. It was not. The pressure continued until we found ourselves unable to sleep, wondering if they were right and if we could live with ourselves if we refused to help when the party was so shattered.

Finally, Ronnie told party officials that if they would make it possible for him to spend the remaining five months of 1965 speaking around the state, he would see for himself if his candidacy offered the best chance of victory. He promised he would give them his answer by December 31. Privately, he thought he would find they were wrong. They employed a political public-relations firm to schedule speeches, and Ronnie began touring what he calls the "mashed potato" circuit in between filming *Death Valley Days* programs. A month or more before the December deadline, he told me he knew our friends were right. We were aware that to go forward would mean a very great change in our lives. We would have to sell the Malibu ranch we loved so much, but maybe we could keep our home in the Palisades. By this time I knew we were facing a responsibility neither of us felt we could turn down.

On December 31 he appeared before a press conference in Los Angeles and announced he would be a candidate. This, of course, did not heal the party's wounds nor unite it. There were those who opposed him simply because he was an actor. His greatest support came (as it did again in 1976) from the grass roots. As one writer put it, "No one wanted him but the people."

The state chairman of the Republican party, who had to remain neutral in what was to be a hard-fought primary, came up with an idea that led to a restoration of party unity. It was the eleventh commandment—"Thou shall not speak ill of another Republican." The Federated Republican Women adopted a resolution that they would not support anyone who violated the commandment, and the race was on.

When the people who were helping run Ronnie's campaign asked if I were willing to help, I said, "Yes, of course," but then the question arose, how? I had never made a speech in my life, and the thought of making one scared me to death. They said, You can stand up and take a bow, can't you? I said I thought I could handle that, so that's what we settled for in the beginning. Little did I dream what I would end up doing.

My first taste of political sniping came when I learned it was being said that my watching Ronnie when he spoke was an act. Well, first of all, I think it is only polite to look at the person who is speaking. Of course, I'll admit I don't look at other speakers the way I look at Ronnie, but I really can't digest what someone is saying unless I look at him or her. Besides, I like to hear Ronnie speak even when I've heard the speech before. I think he's great.

I've often wondered what the remarks would have been if I'd looked at my plate or counted the house while he was speaking.

But it was another example of political sniping that changed my role in campaigning. The campaigning staff came to Ronnie one day and told him the opposing camp was telling people to remember that he was an actor, used to learning lines. Sure, his speeches were good, but who wrote them? Well, he wrote his own but he couldn't go around saying that. He told his helpers the answer was simple: He would shorten his speech by half and throw every meeting open to questions and answers. The audience might think the speech was not his own, but they couldn't doubt the answers were his own. From then on that became his campaign method, and it opened a way for me to do more than listen.

By this time the campaign team had come to know me and had found my soft spot. They pointed out that Ronnie was carrying a heavy load and there wasn't time for him to get to all the places and people who wanted to see and hear him. They said it would really help him a lot if I would make some appearances for him. Of course I said I would, and it was a decision I shall always be happy I made.

I wouldn't have been comfortable giving speeches, but answering questions was a different matter. I found that I enjoyed the give-and-take of a question-and-answer session. I think if you're very shy or if you really don't like people, politics is going to be a terribly hard life for you. I am a little shy but I really do like people, and now we'd found a way in which I could help.

All of us tend to stay in our own little worlds, but a campaign forces you to go places and meet people you would otherwise never have a chance to see and meet. And you learn that the people in this land of ours are pretty wonderful. They are kind and generous and can run their lives without the tender loving care the government would like to give them. They believe that America has gotten off the track somewhere, and is adrift without a rudder or compass. They don't like it. They want to feel as proud of this country as they once did, and they are much stronger than they are given credit for being. In Hollywood I always thought producers tended to underestimate people's intelligence, and now I think most politicians do also.

I believe people are willing to make sacrifices and they long to help if only someone will tell them what they can do. Ronnie has often said he wishes that some day the government would lock its doors and slip quietly away just to see how long it would take the country to miss it.

I was asked many different kinds of questions in that 1966 campaign by a wide variety of people. I learned as much about them and what they felt as they did about me and my feelings. It was a very rewarding experience.

Among the more fascinating places that I visited were college and university campuses. Students often asked me about marijuana. I said I was against it because I thought it was harmful. That was the doctor's daughter in me speaking. I would explain that you can't equate it with alcohol because your body throws off the effects of alcohol while those of marijuana are cumulative and stay in the body. I was surprised at the reaction, though, when I admitted that possibly alcohol had been the crutch of my generation and that they had just chosen a different crutch—marijuana. Then, when I added, "Why not a generation that didn't need any crutch?" I received an ovation.

Now, I'll admit it would have been easy for me to say I didn't object to marijuana simply because I knew that was what the students would have liked to hear, but I didn't and discovered we got along better. They might not have agreed with my answer, but they knew I was honest with them. People are better able to take the truth than politicians realize.

Sometimes I would be asked about the movies being made today and found that most agreed with me that many of them are in bad taste, catering to our worst instincts.

I was asked about, and expressed myself as against, premarital or casual sex, live-in relationships, early marriage and easy divorce, abortions, and permissive child-rearing. Naturally, not everyone agreed with me, and many had good points to make. But the give-and-take was good. Most people basically have moral beliefs and don't want to be "liberated" if this means being liberated away from traditional values.

The only subjects I would not talk about were purely personal ones. I think that each of us has an attitude which shows through. As politely as possible, I made it clear there were areas I would not enter and almost everyone respected this. Again, people have more good sense and sensitivity than they are given credit for. There were a few reporters, especially young ones, who might have been seeking to make names for themselves, who persisted with prying questions, but I resisted and it never really became a problem. Most of the press has treated me well throughout my political days, as has the public.

I've spoken to all kinds of groups and can't say I was ever heckled or treated rudely, even though I'm sure there were some who weren't absolutely in love with me. I never expected to enjoy campaigning as much as I did. I couldn't possibly have emerged from each trip with more respect for the average person, and I'm glad I was given a chance to speak—and to listen.

There is a side to campaigning that can be rough, however: traveling from town to town; hotel rooms with windows that are sealed and can't be opened (which leaves me with a claustrophobic feeling); a strange bed every night; eating and sleeping at strange hours; and banquet menus that usually run to beef or chicken five nights in a row. I've often wondered if anyone has thought of serving just plain stew or Mexican or Chinese food as a welcome change at political dinners.

On the campaign trail everyone gets tired, not just the candidate but those who travel with him—the staff, the press, everyone. I think campaigns last much too long and, as a result, are much too costly. They become an endurance contest. There has to be a better way to show off the candidates and elect our officials.

Ronnie and I always used to travel by train—before politics, that is. We love the privacy and restfulness of train travel. We're both scenery watchers and would sit by the windows for hours, simply looking out. There was always something romantic about trains, and I miss them. You certainly don't feel the same on an airplane, but I guess those days are over.

The first time I took the plane to Sacramento after Ronnie

became governor, Skipper, who was then eight years old, was with me. He had brought his skateboard along. As we neared Sacramento, Skip looked on the floor for the skateboard and couldn't find it. I turned to the man in back of me and asked, "Pardon me, but did you see a skateboard go by?" He looked at me as if I'd taken leave of my senses and very politely turned to the man in back of him and asked, "Did you see a skateboard go by?" The second man said, "Was there anyone on it?" With that, we all started to laugh. The skateboard was finally found at the rear of the plane on the other side of the aisle.

Once, during those first days in Sacramento, I flew to San Diego at a time when Ronnie was having a big fight with the state legislature over the budget. Three men got on, sat directly behind me, and started a heated discussion about his efforts to cut the budget. They were really ripping him apart. As they went on, I could feel myself getting angrier and angrier. Finally, I pushed the button to lower the back of my seat so that I was leaning back literally in their midst. I told them, "That's my husband you're talking about, and more than that, you don't know what you're talking about. He's going to be on television tonight, and if you listen you'll learn all the facts."

Those poor men! I'm sure they wished the floor could have opened up and they could have dropped through. The aide who was traveling with me sank lower and lower in his seat. I think maybe he also wished for a hole to drop into. Come to think of it, he never went on another trip with me.

I think the hardest thing for a wife to take is criticism of her husband. I know that when you're in politics you're bound to be criticized and I don't mind fair, honest disagreement. After all, we have a two-party system, thank God, but if the criticism is unfair or dishonest, then it can hurt terribly, and I'm not really as thick-skinned as I should be. I'm a little better about this than when we first started out, but I'm still not as good as I would like to be. I guess I'm just less surprised by it than I used to be.

Another thing that bothers me is having to listen to political rumors. Many of them are utterly ridiculous. I used to think the film business had a corner on gossip, but it's child's play compared with politics. You are constantly hearing wild stories about what is going to happen to this senator, to that representative, to the governor, or to this bill or that bill. I don't know where all these rumors come from, but there probably are a hundred untrue stories for every one that turns out to be close to the truth.

I found my own way to handle unfair criticism and gossip. I would take long hot baths during which I had marvelous imaginary conversations with people who had said unkind, sometimes vicious, unfounded things. I would think of just the right words to say and the right way to say them. And no one could answer me back. I would get out of the bath feeling terrific. Ronnie says that he could tell when he opened the front door that he'd been in the press just by the smell of the bath salts.

At the risk of sounding like a wife, I would much rather something critical were said about me than about my children or my husband. When I read criticism about him which makes him sound unfeeling and unsympathetic, it really bothers me. He has a motto on his desk that reads, "There is no limit to what a man can do if he doesn't care who gets the credit." I suppose that's true but it's frustrating to know all the warm and compassionate deeds he has performed that are unknown to the public and about which he never speaks.

My husband of twenty-seven years is a man who cannot be measured only by massive accomplishments. He is a man who has kept an important person waiting so he could talk to a child. He is a man who was not so busy being governor that he could not find time to locate summer jobs for needy boys; who indeed found the time to arrange for a movie star to take a dying boy on a visit to Disneyland. He is a man who gave one of his own suits to an eighty-year-old man who didn't have a new suit to get married in; who gave a huge box of yarn in every color of the rainbow to an elderly lady who knits for a living and had no money to buy yarn; who gave an American flag to a Mexican girl named Maria who had just become an American citizen and wanted a flag. He spent sleepless nights because Maria's letter had no return address and he wanted to find her so he could get her the flag. He is a man who has done a hundred things, a thousand things like that.

My husband has deep religious convictions and beliefs. He doesn't parade them openly, but these beliefs are clearly seen in the truly touching letters he often writes to families who have sustained tragedies. He writes these letters himself. They are not written by secretaries or other aides. I'd like to quote from one he wrote to a young man who was disillusioned about his life and his future. Ronnie's secretary sent me a copy of it and I've saved it because I believe it to be quite meaningful:

> Our middle-class, supposedly living in a tight little world, selfish and apathetic, is not really that at all. A great many of them, having failed to realize their own exciting, youthful dreams, have reinvested these dreams in their children, and work and strain to save to provide a better opportunity and a better education so that a son or daughter can achieve the dreams they didn't. Millions and millions of them do more than just earn a living and go home and sit in front of television sets. They are scout leaders, Sunday School teachers, members of clubs that do service and charitable work, and they do what they can, where they can to make things better. While they may not shake the world they keep it from falling apart. Life is not all sordid and seamy, but it is often hard. There is reward for effort, there is penalty for failure. There is much kindness among people, otherwise we wouldn't still be spending billions of dollars on programs to help others even when the programs have proven bungling failures. Life for your generation stretching ahead is very exciting and very joyous because never has the world been so ready for the innovative new ideas for progress and for all the answers to all the ills that beset mankind.

Ronnie, a man who always wanted to make the most of himself, encourages others to do the same. Much as my father always did. Ronnie takes criticism much better than I do. I get much more emotional. He can separate constructive criticism from that which is destructive and what is real from what is of no substance. He takes constructive criticism seriously and listens when there's a real point being made. When he can be shown that he is not entirely in the right, he will modify his stand, but usually he takes enough time on each issue to have thought it through, and when he takes a stand, it's firm.

You learn a lot about a person's character in a campaign and in how he chooses to campaign. Ronnie always has campaigned on the issues and never has attacked anyone personally. Some politicians dodge the issues and launch ruthless personal attacks on their opponents. I don't think people like this and, frankly, I lose all respect for anyone who does it.

On our first election night in 1966, we had dinner with friends and were on our way to the hotel by car when we heard on the radio that Ronnie was the projected winner by about a million votes. I'd always thought that you waited up all night listening to the returns and spent the time biting your fingernails. The results came too fast and I couldn't believe them. Ronnie received 3,700,000 votes, while Pat Brown, although he was the incumbent governor, received only 2,700,000 votes. Therefore, Ronnie won in a runaway by about a million votes. I was overjoyed, of course, but a little letdown, too. Somehow, it seemed it shouldn't have happened in a car; it shouldn't have been heard on the radio. It was almost as if we had been cheated of the delicious suspense we had expected. Of course, if it had been close and we'd had to sweat it out all night, I'm sure we'd have liked that a lot less. That was our first big night, and it was so exciting that it's almost a blur to me now.

We did have the victory celebration at the hotel, where hundreds of Ronnie's supporters had gathered to greet him and cheer him. The bands played and the cheers rang out. Reality set in. The music and cheers died down. The hard work began when he reached Sacramento. As governor, Ronnie did serve wisely and well. The proof came from the public when they voted him a second term in 1970.

But before that happened, we had a different campaign experience, one that has been more misrepresented than almost anything Ronnie has ever done.

The morning after he was elected governor, he and newly elected Lieutenant Governor Bob Finch held a general press conference. Bob was a longtime party worker and had been, once, state chairman of the Republican party.

Almost the first question directed at Ronnie was whether he would be a favorite-son candidate in the 1968 election. If memory serves me correctly, his predecessor had done this in both the 1960 and 1964 presidential elections. Being a favorite son is looked upon as a way of using the state delegation supposedly to benefit the state by helping swing the nomination to the winning candidate. Ronnie replied that he believed in the open primary system.

When it was Bob's turn to take questions, he stated that he hoped he could persuade Ronnie to change his mind. Following the inauguration in January 1967, Bob was joined by party officials and leaders, who pointed out that an open primary so soon after the very divisive 1964 campaign in California could reopen all the wounds that had been healed in the 1966 election. There was no question about the logic of their position, so reluctantly Ronnie went along. However, he insisted that the delegation be representative of every faction in the party. He told them his goal would be to bring back from the convention a delegation still united.

The idea of a favorite-son candidacy is that the presidential candidates will not challenge him in his own state. The 1968 election was beginning to shape up as a contest between Richard Nixon and Nelson Rockefeller in the Republican party. On the Democratic side, Robert Kennedy loomed as the most likely nominee.

In the Republican camp there were many who could not support Rockefeller simply because he had been a participant in the bitter struggle of 1964. At the same time these same people had a great fear that Nixon couldn't win in another Nixon-Kennedy race. Around the country, groups began talking of Ronnie as an alternative and some even announced they would serve as Committees to Nominate Reagan. In every instance Ronnie politely thanked them for the honor they did him and repudiated them at the same time.

Finally, however, he was visited by a delegation representing Republicans from all over the country who said they knew that he would not be an active candidate and would refuse them. However, they asked that he allow his name to be placed in nomination at the convention as a favorite son. Well, of course, to carry out his purpose of bringing back a united delegation, he had to agree with their request. And, beyond that, California law required that this be done. The visiting delegates then told him that they intended to set up a national organization to try and win the Republican nomination for him even though they knew he wouldn't lift a finger as a candidate and that he would have to turn them down.

On the night of California's primary, Robert Kennedy, the Democratic winner, was assassinated. It was a terrible tragedy that all Californians took to heart. Ronnie tried to reach Mrs. Kennedy by phone to see if there was any way that we could help and to offer her every state government resource. In all the confusion the call never got through to her.

At the Republican National Convention in Miami Beach, Richard Nixon was nominated on the first ballot. Ronnie went to the platform immediately to move that the convention make the vote unanimous. Someone tried to stop him on some technicality rule, but National Chairman Ray Bliss said, "To hell with the rules, we want to win an election. Get him to that microphone." The motion carried, and California's delegation returned completely united.

Ronnie never sought the nomination in 1968.

The second campaign was much like the first, except that we knew better what to expect, he had shown he could win, and as an incumbent, he received more support from the party, although it was still the people who really rallied behind him.

There is no way any leader can please everyone, and any leader has to make unpopular decisions at times, so the second election was closer than the first. Even though Ronnie's opponent, Jesse Unruh, was a powerful politician with the support of a strong statewide Democratic party behind him, Ronnie received close to 3,500,000 votes, while Unruh received a little less than 3,000,000. Again we were told of the victory by means of the projections of early returns. Again the bands played and the cheers sounded at the victory celebrations, and with the return to Sacramento, again came the reality of the hard work and accomplishments that could be achieved only with tremendous difficulty.

During the eight years that Ronnie served as governor, our

lives changed beyond anything we had believed possible, and while we could go home again, it never would be quite as it was before.

The campaign trail is a rough road, although, in retrospect, it seems a lot less rough when you find victory at the end of it.

Chapter 7

Ronnie's swearing-in as governor of California took place at one minute after midnight. There have been many wild guesses as to the reason for this. Here is the real one. His predecessor, Governor Pat Brown, had left a great many judicial vacancies unfilled during the election year. Immediately after his defeat he began the wholesale appointment of judges. Every day the press would report another eight or ten appointees. Ronnie became so frustrated he said, "When is the earliest that I can be sworn in?" It turned out to be one minute after midnight following the New Year holiday.

Justice Marshall McComb was asked to do the swearing-in. We invited family, a few friends, including Senator George Murphy (he, too, was an ex-president of the Screen Actors Guild), and Bob Finch, the newly elected lieutenant governor, and his family. We had a mental picture of all of us gathering in the dimly lighted rotunda of the capitol—the brief oath-taking and home to bed. I guess what happened was another example of how our life had changed.

We walked into the capitol rotunda, which was a glare of lights. There were banks of television cameras, and the rotunda, stairs, and balcony were jammed with an overflow crowd. Everyone seemed prepared for this but us. Murph made a few remarks

167

to open the ceremony. After Bob Finch was sworn in, he spoke from a prepared speech. I realized Ronnie had no notes, no prepared speech, but was expected to speak. I thought, My Lord, what's he going to do? We had been so sure that our concept of an informal swearing-in was the way it would be that we hadn't bothered to ask anyone if there were other plans.

Perhaps because of the hour and the fact the Republicans hadn't had a governor in such a long time, it became an extremely emotional moment. The tension was almost unbearable and I was very nervous. Finally, it was Ronnie's turn and he was sworn in. With all the cameras grinding, he turned to Murph and said, "Well, Murph, here we are on the late, late show again." Everyone dissolved in laughter, and it broke the tension.

Ronnie later told me that when he stepped up to the microphone, he didn't have any idea of what he was going to say. I can't remember it all, but I think he spoke about his hopes and plans for the people and the state. Then he paused and turned to the Senate chaplain who had opened the ceremony with an invocation. Ronnie said,

> Reverend, perhaps you weren't a part of my imagining of what this moment would be. But I am deeply grateful for your presence because you remind us and bring here the presence of someone else without whose presence I certainly wouldn't have the nerve to do what I'm going to try to do. Someone back in our history, maybe it was Benjamin Franklin, said if ever someone could take public office and bring to that public office the precepts and teaching of the Prince of Peace, he would revolutionize the world and men would be remembering him for 1,000 years. I don't think anyone could follow those precepts completely. I'm not so presumptuous as to think I can—but I will try very hard. I think it's needed in today's world.

It was a completely impromptu speech but very touching and moving. I was very proud of him and tried hard not to cry.

The inauguration itself was impressive. Reverend Donn Moomaw had come up from Los Angeles to give the invocation, which meant a lot to us. At a concert given by the San Francisco

We attend another Inaugural Ball in Sacramento at the beginning of Ronnie's second four-year term in 1971.

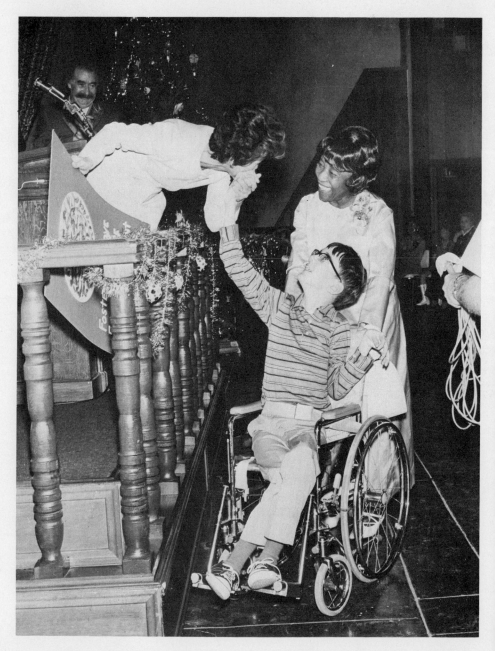

A Foster Grandparent Program visit during the week of Christmas.

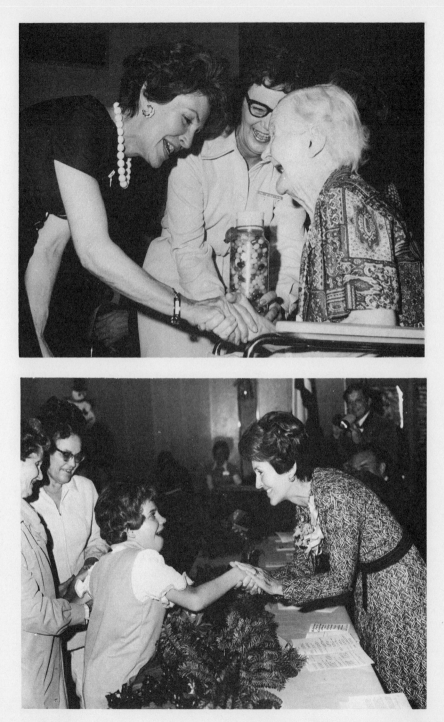

—PHOTO: *Vallejo Times Herald*

I meet an elderly patient at the Arden Memorial Convalescent Hospital in May 1973, and a young lady in Vallejo in connection with the Foster Grandparent Program.

Meeting the men wounded in Vietnam (above).

Greeting one of the POW's at one of the dinners for them (below).

—PHOTO: *Sacramento Bee*

—PHOTO: *Sacramento Bee*

My hugs for Lt. Commander Everett Alvarez, Jr., and Commander Charles Southwick.

Our meeting with President Marcos and Señora Imelda Marcos of the Philippines on the occasion of the opening of the cultural center in Manila.

(Below) Patti and Marcos' daughter get acquainted while we're doing the same in the background.

While on another trip to Asia representing our government, we did some sightseeing in Bangkok's *klongs*, and I found myself being protected from a rabid dog.

On a visit to Rome, Ronnie, Ron and I enjoyed an audience
with Pope Paul VI.

In San Francisco we greeted France's President and
Mme. Pompidou on their official visit to the United States.

Symphony the night before, our dear friend Jack Benny came up and played the violin with the orchestra. The Inaugural Ball was exciting and tiring. After it was all over, we settled down to life in Sacramento—except "settled down" isn't exactly the way it was.

The governor's mansion was built in 1879. It was a Victorian-style house on a street corner with two gas stations and a motel on the other corners. There were no grounds around the house, which backed up to an American Legion hall. It had been condemned as a fire hazard by the fire chief years before. I like old houses, but I'm not crazy about old, *unsafe* houses.

I remember flying to Sacramento to see the mansion after the election. Mrs. Brown gave me a guided tour. She pointed out many of its problems and said if there was anything she could do to help us get a new governor's mansion she would. (Jesse Unruh said the same thing, by the way, at the prayer breakfast before the inauguration.) The Browns had tried to get a new one during his time in office. They had gone as far as choosing an architect and having plans drawn up. But it's my understanding that their projected house was so big and the cost so high, the legislature turned it down. The whole idea had become a political football, which I was never able to understand. It seemed so childish. Governors of both parties would be living in the mansion. What difference did it make which party finally got it done? Still, the result was nothing was being done.

I didn't realize how depressed I was by the tour of the house until I got home and started to tell Ronnie about it. Our own house seemed so cheerful and the mansion seemed so depressing and gloomy that I started to cry. Poor Ronnie, I'm sure I made him feel guilty. I didn't want to do that, but the whole move just suddenly became too much for me. I tried saying I was sure we could do something with it, but I wasn't sure at all.

When we moved in, it was even worse than I thought because we were on the main transcontinental truck route. The trucks roared through constantly, shifting gears at our corner all night long. I defy anyone to be able to sleep in that house. In fact, Mrs. Brown showed me a small back room to which some tenants had retreated in desperation.

The fire hazard really worried me. The place was so old and so filled with dry rot that in a fire it would have gone up like a tinder box. There were seven fireplaces, none of which you could light—by law. There were no fire escapes, only a rope you could throw outside a bedroom window. That was it.

One Friday afternoon The Skipper and I were at home when the fire alarms went off. I grabbed him by the hand and we ran down the stairs, outside. When we had first moved in, we had tried to show young Ron what to do if there were a fire. He was eight years old and we didn't want to frighten him, but felt we should take some precautions. You couldn't budge any of the windows in his room—they were all stuck shut. That Friday I asked the fire marshal what I should tell my son to do. He said, "Well, Mrs. Reagan, tell him to get a dresser drawer, hold it in front of him, run toward the window, break it, and climb out!"

That did it. When Ronnie came home that night, I said, "We're moving! I can't fulfill my obligations to you and the state and leave our son in a house that's unsafe. The only way I can see around this is to move." He said, "Start looking for a house to rent tomorrow." Well, what a stir that created! I was told we couldn't do it—it would be very bad politically. I held out, saying if you tell the people the truth they'll understand. It was another example of politicians underestimating the public because the people did understand, especially the mothers! I think I may have received a half-dozen critical letters but no more than that.

I couldn't help but be amused a few years later when the mansion had been turned into a museum—they wouldn't let visitors upstairs because it was unsafe! But we were supposed to sleep there. I did feel vindicated, I must admit.

I think governor's mansion is a bad term; governor's residence would be better. Whoever the governor is, he has to have somewhere to live with his family, a place that is large enough and nice enough to host official parties and entertain visiting dignitaries. Perhaps the public isn't fully aware how much of this is part of politics. California, being the largest state (in population) in the nation, has a great many visitors. Large sums of money need not be spent hosting guests, but it doesn't seem right to have to send the Vice-President of the United States and his wife down the hall to "Patti's bathroom" as we did, or to have to put heads of state up at local hotels.

As time went on, it became clear the only way California was going to get the governor's residence it needed and deserved would be build it for our successor—whoever that might be. It would have to be made clear that we were not doing it for ourselves. Pat Brown's proposed mansion had been downtown. I didn't feel this area was good for children or really restful for the governor. We found a piece of property in the suburbs overlooking the American River, with lovely old trees and a pretty view. The land was donated to the state so there was no cost to the taxpayers. All the legislature had to do was approve the funds to build the house. It did so. The residence was finished after Ronnie and I left Sacramento. It sits empty and unfurnished now. I never dreamed the new governor would not use it. In any event, the house awaits the next governor and his family.

Meanwhile, we found a suitable house in a residential area away from the heart of town. Although the state is supposed to provide living quarters for the governor, we paid the rent ourselves. When the owners had to sell, friends from both political parties purchased the place, and we rented from them. The house has since been sold. It was in a great neighborhood for kids, so Ron could have the more normal and natural life that I was determined to try to give him. We had a lovely backyard, and Ron built a tree house where he and his friends spent some nights. While security was impossible at the old mansion, it was possible here, and our neighbors benefited from this, too.

We used to entertain the legislature once a year. Since the house wasn't big enough for an indoor function, we'd wait till spring and have the party in the backyard. Some of our friends— Danny Thomas, Red Skelton, Jack Benny—would come and entertain us. It was fun, and when we found the neighborhood kids hanging on the fence to watch, we started inviting them in to sit around the pool, and they had a great time, too.

Because we didn't want to break up our home in the Palisades, we took some of our belongings from the ranch to furnish the new house, and we bought some other things. The rest of the furnishings were donated. I used to scrounge around, begging pieces from people who were breaking up old houses or who might make a donation to the state for a future governor's residence. We got some lovely furniture.

I must admit I wasn't prepared for an attack by Jesse Unruh saying I was collecting these items for myself. He was running for the governorship at the time so I shouldn't have been too surprised, but it brought about my first press conference. I explained that every piece of furniture that had been donated had been accepted by the Director of Finance for the state. The furniture was the state's property, not ours, and would remain so for possible future use in the governor's residence. Sad to say, all those lovely pieces are now in storage in Sacramento waiting to be used.

Not only was the old mansion depressing, but so were the offices at the capitol. It seemed to me the offices of the governor should reflect the dignity of the position and the greatness of our state, and I wanted the people who visited to feel that. I love California, and I wanted it to be presented in the best possible light—especially to the young. I also feel that a man works better if the surroundings are pleasant. These were far from pleasant.

The office was really in disrepair. The carpeting was of all different colors and full of holes. Some holes had been patched, but not always with the same color of carpeting. A leather couch in Ronnie's small office had a large hole in it, with springs poking through. I could go on, but I think you get the general idea.

The first few months I had to split my time between Sacramento and the Palisades—until Ron finished his school semester. I felt terrible leaving Ronnie in a depressing house to go to a depressing office. I thought that for his birthday present I'd fix up the small office he would be occupying for his personal use. Since he took office in January and his birthday was in February, it didn't leave much time. I worked madly. New rich red carpeting had been ordered for the whole governor's wing to add some continuity to it. (The carpeting was already included in the budget before we arrived.) Then I tried to make his room really "his" room. The walls of the study were paneled with a light yellow wood. We stained them a dark color that blended beautifully with the rugs. Ronnie loves horses, so I brought some old English prints we had at home and hung them. The leather couch was repaired and recovered. Some friends gave him a lovely desk for his birthday. We got it done in time. How I'll never know.

The small room opened into a larger room which now, suddenly, seemed worse than before, so I started on it, too. Most of the furniture was donated, and we found some nice paintings for the walls. It became the room where he met with his cabinet.

I think the capitol grounds in Sacramento are the loveliest I've ever seen anywhere, but the blinds in the office were always drawn. Ronnie loves the outdoors and hates a closed-in feeling, so I asked if there were some reason for the drawn blinds. When I was told there was none, we opened them. It made all the difference in the world. Now Ronnie could look out onto the grounds with all the beautiful trees and camellias spread out before his eyes. He was much happier. I remember one legislator coming in, stopping dead in his tracks, and exclaiming, "In all the years I've been here, I never even knew there was a view! It's great."

Well, of course, one room led to another. I must admit I enjoyed the work. The reception room had old-fashioned leather walls. They must have been terribly expensive originally but were outdated now. We replaced them with burlap. I had worked out an arrangement to have paintings by California artists hung on a rotating basis, and this worked out well for the artists and for us.

Then there were the hallways! When we arrived, the only item of decoration was a tomahawk. With the help of some very nice men from the General Services Department, I found some old prints that had been stashed away at Fort Sutter. Some had almost disintegrated, but they were marvelous, fascinating pictures of the early days in Sacramento, San Francisco, and Los Angeles; the legislature in the 1800's; the capitol in various stages when it was being built; and so forth.

In the years that followed, it did my heart good to see tour groups go by. They always stopped and looked closely at the prints. As a matter of fact everyone did, which made for quite a jam up in the halls! All appeared delighted with them. I was especially pleased that young people found them interesting and were able to take away with them a little of the history of the state. The feeling on the part of the visitors was that the wing was warmer and brighter and more interesting than before. I had spent very little money. The legislature seemed satisfied. The press reported the improvements favorably. As a frustrated interior decorator, I was really pleased. It was one of my better birthday presents to Ronnie.

Our life changed drastically, of course. Only the President of the United States has more responsibilities to more people than the governor of a state the size of California. The pressures are tremendous and the problems so complex that they sometimes seem beyond solution. I did whatever I could to ease the load on Ronnie.

Patti was away at school, but Ron was with us at home, and I felt it was important to try to keep as much of a family life as possible. We had breakfast together every morning and dinner every night, except for those times Ronnie and I had to go to some function or other. There were nights when he was so tired he didn't want to talk, but there were other times when he did want to discuss an idea or a situation that had gone on during the day. I was his sounding board. It's nice to have someone at home just to listen to you. Many times just talking out a problem provides the solution you've been looking for.

I must say we really walked into the "turbulent Sixties." The students were demonstrating on campuses, rioting against authority, burning property. As I look back on it, what a sad time for them! The four years of college are a precious and special interlude that can never be relived, and it was all wasted for so many of them. There was no joy, no fun, no laughter.

Ronnie hadn't created the problems, but he had to solve them. The campuses had to be closed briefly at one time to restore order. He could not and would not condone violence or give in to force. He felt education provided by the state was a privilege, and the price you paid for it was decent behavior, respect for others, and hard work.

Sadly, he lost the young for a while. Hatred is a terrible thing to see, but on the faces of young people it's especially heartbreaking. It was horrible to hear the language they put on their signs and shouted. We were paying for the age of permissiveness in which many children had been allowed to do whatever they wanted, to have their own way—whatever the price. That, of course, was not true of all students. Some just went to their classes, did their work, and took no part in the demonstrations. How they did it I'll never know. My hat is off to them. It must have been very difficult for them and have taken a lot of courage.

Some of the complaints were justified. I think that many of the campuses are too large. The student just becomes a number and has little or no contact with instructors. Too many courses don't satisfy the needs of the students. These are legitimate problems which should be faced. In any event, it's a pleasure to see peace on the campuses again and joy on youthful faces, and to find learning and studying taking the place of riots. Ronnie again enjoys the empathy with youth he had before and is very happy about it. I think his problems with the young bothered him almost more than anything else during his time in Sacramento.

Of course, one of the most painful duties a governor can have is the power of life or death over another human being. Aaron Mitchell had been sentenced to die at San Quentin prison in May 1965. It became the responsibility of the governor to decide finally whether or not the death sentence should be upheld. A man's life should not be taken without a lot of soul-searching and serious investigation into the case. Ronnie did all of those things and finally decided the verdict was right. Aaron Mitchell was executed in April 1967. This is the last execution that has taken place in California even though other men have since been sentenced to death.

Ronnie and I both believe in the death penalty and are convinced it is a deterrent to murder, that individuals are alive today because of it. In California the majority of people believe as we do and have voted to have the penalty put back on the books.

Mitchell's execution was to be at ten in the morning. The night before, there was an all-night vigil at our house. It was a silent vigil, with the protestors peacefully carrying candles. I remember eight-year-old Ron watching this rather eerie scene through the window and wondering about it. We tried to explain to him the necessity for his dad to have decided as he did and about the good intentions of those who protested. It was a long night indeed. One of the things the protesters wanted was for all the church bells to ring at ten o'clock the following morning so that everyone could pray for Aaron Mitchell's soul. I had no argument with that. However, I think it would be nice if they could also ring church bells every time someone is murdered so that we could pray for their souls, too. I wonder if the protesters ever knew that at exactly ten o'clock, Ronnie called me from his office and that together we, too, prayed for Aaron Mitchell.

A little later, Ronnie received a letter from an elderly man in San Francisco, who ran a little "Mom and Pop" store with his wife. He thanked Ronnie for saving his life. He told him they had been robbed a few days after the execution—which had, of course, received a lot of press. One of the robbers had knocked him to the floor and tried to stab him. He had held on to the robber's wrist, but the knife came closer as his strength gave out. Desperately, he shouted, "You'll get the gas chamber if you do." The robber hesitated for a moment and then fled. This story reinforced our feeling that the death penalty is truly a deterrent. It made the memory of that long night easier to bear.

There were many things Ronnie did during his two terms as governor that I was proud of—especially since he had to do it the hard way, with a legislature primarily composed of members of the other political party. He took a bankrupt state and put it on a sound fiscal basis. As surpluses developed, he saw to it they were returned to the taxpayers in tax refunds, credits, lowered bridge tolls, and the like. All told, he returned $5.7 billion to the people. He reformed welfare so that cheaters were not allowed to take advantage of the program and the truly needy received the money they deserved. As a matter of fact, they got a forty-three percent average increase in their welfare grants.

He completely reformed the mental-health programs in order to end the so-called warehousing of mentally ill or retarded people in huge old institutions. The programs were broken down into smaller treatment centers, and out-patient-type treatment was developed wherever possible so these patients could adapt to as normal a life as possible. This system became a model program of its kind, and other states sent specialists to California to study it and copy it.

When Ronnie first took office, one of the first things I was asked was what my pet project would be, as if I had prepared some program which would be helpful politically. I've done a lot of different work for a lot of causes, and I presumed I would continue to do so, but I couldn't say one stood out above the others. In time, I did find one—but it developed naturally and was not a calculated effort on my part. Being a doctor's daughter and having been a nurse's aide, I had a natural interest in visiting hospitals. I went to all kinds—for the young, the elderly, the mentally retarded, the men home from wars. If you ever feel sorry for yourself, try visiting hospitals. I'm sure I got much more out of this experience than I could possibly have given.

I've always felt most programs benefit only one side, but one day I visited Pacific State Hospital and saw a project called "The Foster Grandparent Program." I was deeply impressed. As the day went on, I became more so. Here was a program in which both sides benefited: the elderly who served as "grandparents" and the children. Old people often experience a point in their lives, after their children are grown and gone, when they feel lonely, unwanted, unneeded, and unloved (those things we all may feel someday). Yet, they still have so much to give. In the other half of the equation were the mentally retarded children who need a great deal of attention and love—more than any hospital can possibly provide. Bring these two groups together, and each gives what the other needs. I got involved in the program and got Ronnie to back it. It was a marvelous and rewarding experience.

The program gives the elderly a whole new life, a reason for getting up in the morning, and a purpose in living. They have a lot to give, especially a lot of love that's been bottled up inside. The elderly are effective because of their age and all those traits only experience can bring. They are more patient than many younger people, less discouraged by seemingly small, slow results,

185

and much more tolerant. The children, of course, respond immediately to extra love and attention. In many instances the elderly are the only family these children have or ever will have. Their regular daily contact with the Foster Grandparents makes a big difference in their lives.

I've had many letters from the Grandparents saying how much the program has meant to them, how before they had had nothing and no one to care for. This has opened up a whole new world for them. One woman wrote, "You told us we were important and doing something worthwhile, so we sort of sat back and grinned at ourselves since we were being useful at 60 or 80. We'll strive now to be even better." In order to participate in the program, the Grandparents must be in good health. They undergo regular physical examinations and are asked to give four hours a day, five days a week. They are paid a small sum by the hour plus travel costs, and they get a free lunch. I think, however, they would do it for nothing because it means so much to them.

My first day at Pacific State Hospital began with a husky Oriental boy named George, who took me by the hand and never let go for the whole day. Wherever I went, he went. When I had to leave, he started to cry. So did I.

I couldn't wait to tell Ronnie about my discovery of this new program which was small, not widespread, or well-funded. He agreed with me about its value. We helped expand it to all state hospitals. It was picked up by ACTION, the volunteer-service agency, so it received more funds. The Foster Grandparent Program gradually spread into other states. We now have expanded the service so that it includes not only the retarded but the deaf and juvenile delinquents. I am proud of it and of all the Grandparents. It's been a bit like watching your baby grow up and mature. It has become my pet project and always will be. I am as pleased at whatever part I have played in its success as I am of anything I have ever done.

Still, in all my hospital visits I think I have been as touched by the wounded veterans as by anything else. They usually wanted to talk about what had happened to them in battle. I was overwhelmed by how simply and humbly they described acts of bravery, the matter-of-fact manner in which they told about the ordeals they had endured. I learned that one little word or sentence could trigger tears, and I'd have to hold on tight not to break up. Sometimes I did and would have to disappear behind a door until I could regain control.

In those first years, 1967 and 1968, both Ronnie and I were overwhelmed by the job the armed services had done in motivating these young men. Time after time we'd hear a multiple amputee (there was a higher percentage of these wounded than in any other war) tell us he was convinced of the rightness of our cause and that his only regret was that he couldn't rejoin his outfit. The veterans expressed great sympathy and friendship for the Vietnamese people. But as the Vietnam War ground on, I began to notice a difference in the attitudes of some—a bitterness that we weren't winning. Along with Ronnie, I believe it was wrong—immoral—that our government asked these young men to fight and die for their country without letting them win. This should never be allowed to happen again.

I agreed to write a question-and-answer column for the newspapers on condition that the payment go to the National League of Families of American Prisoners of War and Missing in Action. I corresponded with, talked to on the phone, and met many of the mothers, wives, and children of these men, and became very close to this cause. The women were truly amazing. In many cases they did not know whether their husbands were dead or alive, but they never gave up hope. They assumed all responsibilities for their families and carried on.

When the wives first formed the POW-MIA organization, Ronnie had a press conference in his office to help inform the people of California. He felt a tug on his pants leg and looked down to see a little boy trying to get his attention. Ronnie leaned down, and the little boy whispered, "Will you help bring my daddy home?" As you can imagine, it was a little difficult for Ronnie to continue talking. Soon there was another tug. He bent down again, and, with all the TV cameras going, the little boy said, "I have to go to the bathroom." Everyone broke up; Ronnie and the boy excused themselves. As it turned out, the boy's dad never came home, but later his mother married another POW and they are all very happy.

* * *

Along with millions of other Americans, we sat in our home and watched—tears streaming down our faces—the first of the flights bringing the POW's home. I had a lump in my throat the size of a basketball. We held our breath, but when the plane door opened and Jeremiah Denton stepped through, smiled, saluted the flag, made his way down the ramp unaided, and ended his short remarks with "God Bless America," we knew everything was going to be all right.

Each man who followed saluted the flag and was greeted by his family. By this time, I could have floated away in a sea of tears, and I turned to Ronnie and said, "If I don't have a chance to put my arms around them I'm going to pop. We've got to do something." Ronnie agreed, and thus were born the four dinners we gave—two at our home in Sacramento for those who came from the north and two in our Los Angeles home for those in the south. I wanted to have these parties in the warmth of a home and not in a hotel ballroom. I told the returnees to bring anyone they wanted—wife, mother, sister, girlfriend—or just come alone. They were welcome any way they wanted it.

The first dinner in Sacramento was the most memorable. The men had been home only a few days, and emotions were running high. The children and neighbors heard about it and lined up on both sides of the walk waiting for them to come. First came the men who had been held prisoner the longest and so were the first to be brought back. Lieutenant Commander Everett Alvarez, Jr., who had been imprisoned the longest of all, was present, as was Commander Dick Stratton, one of the highest-ranking officers held captive. So were many others. I can't name them all. Each one got the hug I had wanted to give. Commander Charles Southwick was there and said he had something for me. The "something" was the tin spoon from which he'd eaten for seven years in captivity. I dissolved, of course. It was a very wet evening—all in all—but one I'll never forget.

The returnees told stories that were so harrowing it was unbelievable, and we wondered how anyone could live through such tortures. Some had been physically broken, but few had been spiritually broken. They told of the mental games they had played to keep from losing their sanity, and of devising complicated communication systems which consisted of taps between cells.

We actually saw two men meet in our living room, hear each other's name, and throw their arms around each other. They were the closest friends—knew everything about each other's family. They met face-to-face for the first time in their lives there in our home. Their friendship had been forged during their years of captivity when they occupied adjoining cells and communicated by tapping on the wall in code.

Always at some point during the dinner someone would stand and toast us. *They* toasted *us*! The reverse of what it should have been! We toasted them, of course, and said we would forever be in their debt and could never repay them for what they had given up for us. Lieutenant David Rehman told Ronnie, "You were the last man I voted for." He had been captured even before Ronnie was sworn in. Captain Lee Profilet was there, and his was one of the ID bracelets Ronnie had worn.

We've gone to each of their reunions. At the last one I told them I still have everything they gave me: The tin spoon, of course; a pair of lieutenant bars; even a package of Vietnamese cigarettes; every letter, every poem; I'll treasure each, always. When anyone asks me what was the high point of my husband's administration, I tell them this was it. I love all those returned POW's and have the highest respect for them. They will always occupy a very special place in my heart.

I'm sorry politics is such a dirty word these days. We need good men, badly—especially now. One thing that happens to a wife when her husband takes a position of power is that she gets to see him in different circumstances of stress than the average wife and so gets a better reading of him than do most. Ronnie makes for good reading. I have been lucky because what I always suspected about him I found out was absolutely true.

The families of men in power, however, find they live in a fishbowl. This can be unnerving, to say the least. Some of the pressures placed on your man press on you, too, and you have to be strong to stand them. I had to learn to live with the thought and possibility of danger. But you take all the precautions you can, and then put faith in God and go about your daily life. If you don't, you can't function.

During the time in 1968 when Ronnie was a favorite-son candidate, Secret Service agents had been assigned to us as they had to several others following the tragic assassination of Robert Kennedy. They were wonderful men, and we became close friends with them.

One night we were in bed when we heard a sound that Ronnie said was a shot. He got up, put on a robe, and went out in the hall. A young Secret Service man carrying a shotgun was on the stairs and said very politely, "Governor, would you mind not getting in front of any windows." It seems that one of the agents saw two men trying to light a Molotov cocktail beneath our windows. The agent got off one shot—the one we'd heard—but didn't dare fire again as the men ran to a car and took off. They left the unlighted fire bomb behind. Usually those things are Coke bottles filled with gasoline. Ours was a magnum-sized champagne bottle. It doesn't take much imagination to figure what our chances would have been if that had come through the window.

Ronnie, in discussing the incident with the press, described the shot that was fired as a warning shot. Later, the agent told him, "Governor, we don't fire warning shots. I just missed, and I couldn't fire again because of all the houses around here."

I've never asked about threats on our lives. I don't know how many there have been and I don't want to know. I always knew something was brewing, though, because there would suddenly be more security men around than usual. The only incident I was made aware of—accidentally—was one I heard about on TV. It was a threat against me personally, and I must say that it rattled me. It rattled Ronnie even more. The plot was to kidnap me and send Ronnie my head if he wouldn't agree to release certain individuals from prison.

I guess every step in life prepares you for the next, however, and I believe I learned a lot from all of my steps. At least, I hope I have. The presidential campaign in 1976 included dangers that were greater than ever, pressures that were heavier than ever, and a life that was made more hectic than ever.

If we are ever going to restore faith in our elected leaders and return to a feeling of pride in our country, then those who have the opportunity to serve should take it. I feel Ronnie is lucky to be one of those chosen, and I feel lucky to be along for the ride. It's a little like riding on a roller coaster. It scares you half to death at times and you are not sure you will get through it, but when it's over you feel that it was surely worth it.

Chapter 8

I remember clearly my last few hours at the governor's residence in Sacramento. For weeks I had been packing and supervising the move. This piece of furniture went to the state, that piece to the ranch, and that one to our home in Pacific Palisades. It was so hectic I hadn't had time to dwell on leaving. Suddenly, I was sitting alone in our dark bedroom at twilight, surrounded by packed bags, waiting for Ronnie to pick me up. All the furniture was gone. After eight years of excitement, I sat in silence, waiting to leave. It was a lonely feeling. I wondered if others before me had found themselves sitting in a dark, empty room, feeling as lonely as I did.

Ronnie came and, after a tearful farewell to the girls who worked at the residence, we went to a reception given in our honor by everyone who had worked for us. It was a little like leaving our family—very emotional and weepy. We were both very moved by it. They gave us a painting—a California landscape—which we treasure, but that was the least of the good things they gave us over the years. We left a lot of good friends behind in Sacramento, some of whom are not in politics and don't move in the same circles, and so, sadly, we don't see them much anymore. I had grown attached to our house and the beautiful garden with the flowers I loved, but it was time to go. The door shut behind us, we were gone, and it was all left behind.

I don't know if you leave your mark on a house. I know our son Ron did. When his books were removed from the bookcase, I saw that on the back of the case he had scratched "Ronnie Reagan Slept Here" and dated it, for posterity's sake. I know his father left his mark in Sacramento. I think he may have been the first governor who tried to do exactly what he said he wanted to do, and I think he accomplished more than most. He conducted a clean administration and inspired a lot of people to reach for the heights.

I looked forward to life slowing down for us and more time together, but it didn't happen. First, we had to reestablish ourselves at our homes in Pacific Palisades and Santa Barbara, where we had purchased our new ranch, which needed fixing up. Then, it turned out Ronnie had greater demands on his time than ever before because everyone assumed he had more time than before. He started to write a newspaper column, broadcast a daily radio commentary, and give speeches across the country. To this day, he hasn't stopped.

I think most people assumed he had his eyes on the presidency, but that isn't so. He'd been mentioned as a possible presidential candidate from the time he took office in Sacramento, but he didn't campaign for the office until 1976 and never really talked seriously about it until then. As far as I could see, he was satisfied to live his life and let developments take care of themselves. I think he felt frustrated by the things he hadn't been able to do in Sacramento. One man can only do so much, though he had done more than most. A lot of good ideas get tangled up in the spider web of politics, and there was much that he wanted to see done for America. So, he took the opportunity to continue speaking his mind. He had been fighting the good fight for a long time and wasn't about to stop.

From the time Ronnie became governor to the present, we've taken trips around the world, either on our own or as representatives of our government. With all the minuses of public life, for me, this has certainly been a big plus. I've had the opportunity

A meeting with Billy Graham.

Our farewell to Sacramento after eight years.

I'll never forget visiting a children's hospital in Dallas during the 1976 campaign.

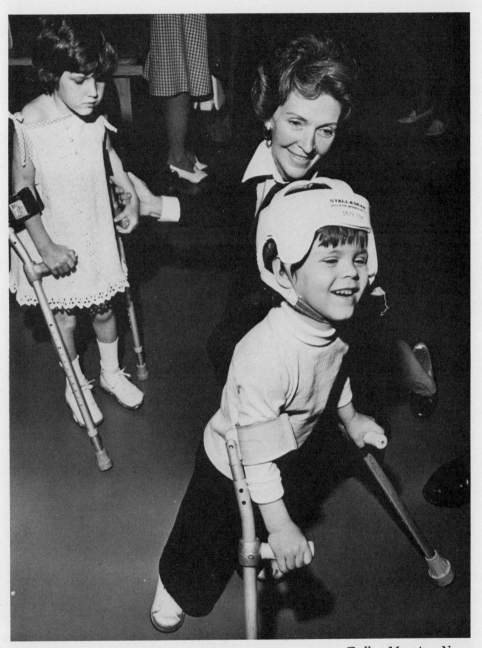

—PHOTO: CLINT GRANT, *Dallas Morning News*

In the photograph above, the two children are Donna Marie Schmidt and Kevin Colcote.

—PHOTO: *Dallas Morning News*

As a part of the campaign excitement I was given baseballs by Gaylord Perry and an autographed football by Thomas "Hollywood" Henderson of the Dallas Cowboys. I thought of them as my good luck charms.

The exciting night of the California primary.   —PHOTO: © MICHAEL EVANS

Ouch! Someone really had a firm, firm grip.
—PHOTO: WALTER ZEBOSKI, AP

Everyone teased me for always being wrapped up in a blanket on the campaign flights.

—PHOTOS: WALTER ZEBOSKI, AP

My response to the demonstration for Ronnie during the 1976
GOP convention in Kansas City. (L. to r.) Barney Barnett, Colleen,
and Ron are with me, with Mike Wallace right behind.

—PHOTO: TONY KORODY, SYGMA

The last night in Kansas City, just before Ronnie was called down to the platform to address the convention.

—PHOTO: TONY KORODY, SYGMA

to travel to places I never would have been able to before and to meet people I never dreamed I would meet. It's been fascinating and enlightening. I feel that I learned and grew from the experiences, and I'm happy our children could be on some of the trips.

On five occasions we were asked to represent the President on missions abroad. The first time we did so was more ceremonial than diplomatic. We attended the formal opening of the great new cultural center in Manila, a project of the Philippines' First Lady Imelda Marcos. We were flown there in one of the Air Force planes assigned to the White House, and were the guests of President Marcos during our stay at the 400-year-old palace which is the official resident of the president of the Philippines.

On each of these trips, the Secret Service accompanied us, as well as a State Department representative and, of course, a few of our own staff. And speaking of staff, I should mention one person in particular who became much more than that. Nancy Reynolds became my close friend and right arm. We were together so long we began to think alike, and she could almost anticipate what I was going to say or do. We could spark ideas off each other, which made not only for a very workable combination but a very happy one. So many funny things have happened to us both that it would take another book to tell them all. In addition, she was most efficient and capable.

Nancy used to accompany me on the visits to the military hospitals when Ronnie couldn't go. She had me pegged pretty well. On one of those visits, I overheard her advising the officer in charge he'd have to tell me when my time was up or I'd stay all day and all night. But I have her pegged, too—she's just as sentimental as I am. Anyway, the trips wouldn't have been the same without her.

Two years after that visit to the Philippines, we were invited to visit Japan as guests of the Japanese government. Our own President had asked Ronnie to extend the trip and represent our government in several other places. This trip was definitely not ceremonial. Dr. Henry Kissinger was in Peking making final arrangements for President Nixon's historic journey to mainland China. We went to Taiwan where Ronnie explained the purpose of the President's China visit to Generalissimo Chiang Kai-shek, and where we represented our government at the celebration of the Double Ten (the anniversary of the Nationalist Chinese overthrow of the Manchu dynasty). We met with Generalissimo and Madame Chiang at their home, and truly felt a sense of history being in their presence.

From Taiwan our mission took us to Singapore to meet with the dynamic Prime Minister Lee. Then, on to Thailand and beautiful Bangkok for meetings with government officials and with the king.

Of course, we did some sightseeing also, even though the trips were definitely official business. One morning in Bangkok we got up at 5 A.M. to go down the *klongs*, which are canals that serve as streets. They are lined with houses and stores right to the water's edge. At that early hour we saw people washing their teeth, squatting on steps that led down to the water, while next door a neighbor was rinsing dishes in the same water.

Bangkok has its own version of our supermarkets: canoes lined up side-by-side with every kind of merchandise, from foodstuffs to clothing. The customers also paddle about in canoes, doing their shopping.

There is a tradition in Bangkok that if you build a house you are disturbing the spirits who occupied the land before your house was built. To keep them from harming you, a little spirit house is erected on a spot where the shadow of the larger house cannot fall on it. These spirit houses can be as elaborate as you can afford. I was enchanted with them and, thinking there might be a few bad spirits in Sacramento I'd like to be protected from, we asked our boatman to steer us to a shop besides the *klongs* where we could buy one. (Nancy Reynolds also bought one.) But it almost turned out to be my last trip. As I was helped to the dock, I headed for an old woman who was presiding over quite a stock of spirit houses. I didn't see the dog at her side until Ed Hickey (the chief of our security) had his arm around me pulling me back, and I realized he'd drawn his gun. The dog was frothing at the mouth—he was rabid. Fortunately, he did not attack us.

We brought the spirit house back to Sacramento, where it sat in the garden. We now have it in the Palisades, where I hope it's doing its duty and warding off all those bad spirits, as a good spirit house should!

After Bangkok we flew on to Vietnam, where security was very tight. Ronnie was taken by helicopter directly to the palace in Saigon for a meeting with President Thieu. Ron and I were taken to the ambassador's house for lunch, also by helicopter. We landed on the rooftop guarded by men with machine guns. We were whisked away down a stairway into a car with the curtains drawn. Never having been in Saigon, I couldn't resist peeking out and saw what used to be a lovely French town. You could certainly see the influence from the decades when Vietnam was part of French Indochina.

At lunch I was amazed at how calm the Vietnamese women were, while my heart was going like a trip-hammer. I suppose if you have to live with a situation like that day after day, you learn to develop a calmness, otherwise you'd never be able to cope!

After our return, I was saddened to hear that the husband of one of the pretty Vietnamese women we lunched with had been murdered. Someone had put a bomb underneath his car. I often wonder whatever happened to her and her children. We returned to the airfield by the same route and met some of our soldiers. I took down some more names so that I could make some "Nancy-who?" calls when I got back.

There, as elsewhere, I visited the hospitals. Wherever there were wounded Americans, I went to see them. If a visit from me would mean anything to those boys, I wanted to give them that. At the hospitals, you'd find out what war is, there and in the cemeteries. So I tried not to cry. I tried to cheer up the boys, and bring them news from home, as well as take news home with me. I'd take names and phone numbers, and when I got home, I'd make the calls:

"Hello, this is Nancy Reagan . . ."

"Nancy who?"

"Nancy Reagan, Ronald Reagan's wife. The governor's wife."

"Oh sure . . ."

"Really. I was in Vietnam and I visited with your son in the hospital there and he asked me to call. . . . He's fine. . . . He really is. . . . He's doing well. . . . He wanted you to know . . ."

"You really are Nancy Reagan . . ."

Then we'd cry a little, together. We were in this together. We all were parents. These were our children.

From Saigon we went on up the coast of Asia to Seoul, Korea, to meet with President Park. Our course took us just offshore North Vietnam, and we couldn't help wondering if our plane with its insignia and large American flag might not be a tempting target for a few MIG fighter planes. The trip was uneventful, however, and a few hours later we were in South Korea.

In the United States there are many who portray President Park as unduly harsh and dictatorial, but when you stand in Seoul—a thriving modern city based on free enterprise—and look northward only sixteen miles to the Communist enemy, you wonder if that's a valid evaluation. With no language or ethnic barrier between the two Koreas, Communist infiltration is very easy. This was tragically evident when President Park's wife was killed in an assassination attempt on her husband while he was addressing a public meeting.

Just before our arrival, there was rioting on the campus of the University of Seoul. It was interesting to see how such things are handled in these countries. First, let me say there was irrefutable evidence that the rioting was engineered by Communist infiltrators. The president simply closed the university, and the young men were drafted into the army. President Park told Ronnie that after they had a little taste of military life, he'd reopen the university, and he was sure the returning students would have a greater appreciation of their educational opportunity.

We had a few busy but enjoyable days in South Korea, then proceeded to Tokyo, where we were the invited guests of the Japanese government. Ronnie addressed several groups and met with the prime minister, as well as a number of other cabinet members. We both had an unprecedented audience with the emperor and empress of Japan. Prior to this they had only received heads of state. The royal couple were utterly charming and kind, and we found ourselves completely at ease with them.

Before leaving Japan, we took the Bullet train (130 miles per hour) to the ancient city of Kyoto, where we visited the fabulously beautiful temples, gardens, and palaces of the early samurai warlords. We then journeyed by automobile to Osaka, a bustling industrial city, where Ronnie and Ron went through one of Japan's great ship-building plants.

Ron turned out to be a great traveler. We had worried that he might dig in his heels when faced with foreign food, but he fooled us. He insisted on trying every dish native to the countries we visited. We learned that the Secret Service agents who were to take care of him when we were involved in some state dinner or affair eagerly volunteered for the assignment. It seems they had a lot more fun with him, going places and seeing things they'd never had a chance to visit or see in their normal routine.

Our next and probably most important diplomatic mission came in 1972. The President had completed his historic visit to Red China and was now scheduled to meet with Leonid Brezhnev and other Soviet leaders in Moscow. It was a time of some discontent and worry among our NATO allies; they needed reassurance that we were not going it alone and that NATO was indeed our most important line of defense.

We visited seven countries in Europe, meeting with heads of state, foreign ministers, industrial leaders, etc. You really learn about jet lag on journeys like this! Our first stop was Denmark, a nine-hour time difference from California. You meet with the prime minister at 4 P.M., his time, the very next day, which is 1 A.M. in the morning your time. You try to remember that yawning in the prime minister's face is hardly the diplomatic thing to do, but inevitably you yawn.

In Denmark a portion of the visit was devoted to ceremony, a very wonderful and moving ceremony. We journeyed with our fine Ambassador Fred Russell to the city of Rebild for a Fourth of July celebration. Each year (for seventy-five years at a time) our Fourth of July is celebrated in Denmark by the Rebild Society, an organization devoted to recognizing the bond that exists between our two countries by reason of the Danes who have become

Americans. Many Americans of Danish descent return each year to Rebild to celebrate our Independence Day. The ceremony is held in a valley and attended by the royal family, representatives of our government (in this case, us), and more than 40,000 people, who gather on the steep hillsides. Much to our surprise and delight, we discovered that Danny Kaye had been invited to appear on the program. In addition to a Danish band, we were greeted by an American high-school band that had been touring Europe. It was quite a moment when both bands played the two national anthems, and the flags of Denmark and the United States were raised on twin flagpoles.

The only interruption in this celebration occurred when the Nazis occupied Denmark during World War II. But even then, we learned that as dawn would break on each July 4, there on the hills surrounding Rebild the American and Danish flags could be seen flying atop two poles. The Nazis would blast them down with artillery fire, but the next Fourth of July they'd have to do it again. To this day, no one has ever revealed who raised those flags or how they did it.

The following day we lunched on the queen of Denmark's beautiful sailing yacht, and then were on our way to Belgium, where we had tea with the king and queen and Ronnie had a day-long briefing at NATO headquarters. Ronnie has never forgotten a birthday or anniversary, but this July 6 we got up, had breakfast, and he never said a word. I thought, "Hm, maybe the rules are different when you're out of the country or something," so I never said anything, but I should have remembered Nancy Reynolds. When we got to the plane, everyone was on board and they all yelled "Surprise." The plane was all decorated inside with balloons, colored paper, and pictures. Somewhere between Denmark and Brussels, we had champagne and a birthday cake. It was a wonderful surprise party—and certainly a different one. I was grateful to Nancy, but also happy Ronnie hadn't forgotten after all!

I think I should point out that while I'm reminiscing about these visits and dwelling on the fun times, the trips had a serious purpose. There were endless hours and days of meetings, and Ronnie spent the hours in flight poring over briefing books that had been provided by Henry Kissinger.

But if you don't mind, I'm going to keep telling about the extracurricular experiences that stick in my memory. I'm a sightseer at heart, and when we had lunch at 10 Downing Street in London, I kept imagining all the others who had been there before us. When we went to Versailles, I kept thinking, "Oh, if these walls could talk!" Monsieur and Madame Gerald Van der Kemp (Monsieur Van der Kemp is the curator at Versailles who has done such a marvelous job of restoring it) gave a lovely dinner for us there where we met the Duke and Duchess of Windsor. The Duke was remarkably well informed about Ronnie's activities and philosophy (and in agreement with it). The Duchess was Ronnie's dinner partner and such a charmer I could see why a man would give up his throne for her.

The Van der Kemps had arranged for us to have a private tour of Versailles with Madame Ehrlich, a wonderful elderly woman who had been living there for years but who is dead now, unfortunately. Madame Ehrlich was so steeped in French history she truly made it come alive for us. She showed us the marks on the stairs made by the boots of the revolutionaries who came to take Marie Antoinette to her death. The captain of the soldiers, guarding her bedroom, died trying to save her. Even the revolutionaries took her out the back way rather than let her see the bloodstained hall and stairs. The stairs are still there! As Madame Ehrlich talked, she made us see, feel, and sense every moment of that episode. I was breathless with excitement. I wish our children had teachers like that. What a difference it would make in their interest in history!

This European trip included, in addition to Denmark and Belgium, France, Spain, Italy, England, and Ireland. We had an audience with the Pope; a meeting with Generalissimo Franco and with the king and queen of Spain, who are now the official heads of state; and dinner with the commander of our Sixth Fleet in the Mediterranean.

You know, when you are accompanied by security men, you get out of the habit of carrying money. You don't stop to pay the hotel bills or even restaurant checks. The security people want to keep you moving, so they pay the checks. Of course, the bill is presented to you later on for settlement.

When we left the United States, Ronnie had a five dollar bill, a dime, and a penny in his pocket. One night in Paris, when as it happened there was no state dinner, Nancy Reynolds arranged that Ronnie, Ron, and I have dinner at Maxim's. There were, of course, Secret Service men at another table who would pay the check when dinner was over. There was one thing, however, we hadn't anticipated; Maxim's features a strolling violinist who walks through the restaurant pausing at each table and usually picking up a dollar tip at each one. This evening, he was coming toward our table. Ronnie asked me if I had any money and, of course, I didn't. Then he asked Ron if he had a dollar on him. Ron looked at him and said, "You have got to be kidding." Ronnie said to us, "Keep eating, don't look up. Maybe he won't stop." Well, he did stop and played a full chorus of "California, Here I Come." Everyone in the room applauded. Ronnie just reached in his pocket and handed him the five-dollar bill!

Our last day abroad was spent viewing the ruined castle on Cashel Rock in Ireland—the place where St. Patrick erected the first cross on Irish soil. The castle is on a hill with a lovely view and is truly beautiful. Ed Hickey and I decided we could be happy if we lived there, knowing that's where we'd be buried. We had a delightful Irish guide, who finally brought us to an iron gate. He explained that the castle perched on its limestone rock was able to withstand a siege because of a well that tapped an underground stream whose source was a lake miles away in the hills. With a flourish he threw open the iron gate, revealing the well, and said, "'Tis a wishing well." Ronnie sighed, reached in his pocket and gave me the dime; he took the penny and we threw both coins in the well. He now says we toured Europe on $5.11.

While we were in Spain, we were driven from Madrid to Toledo, where we visited the Alcazar, a fortress which is to the Spanish what, in a way, the Alamo is to us.

During the Spanish civil war, the Communist forces had surrounded Toledo. The people took refuge in the underground corridors and dungeons of the Alcazar, where they held out for weeks while the fortress above them was reduced to rubble by artillery fire.

We were shown a room aboveground still bearing the scars of war. It had been the commanding officer's headquarters. The room had a glass case containing a telephone, and on the wall above hung two oil paintings, one of an older man, the other of a strikingly handsome youth. There was also a plaque explaining the pictures and the phone.

The civil war had been a little unusual in that the phone lines were still intact. The Communist attackers could telephone the Alcazar. One day the commander of the fortress (the older of the two men in the paintings) received a call from the Communist commander. He was told they had his son (the youth in the other portrait) and that if he didn't surrender the Alcazar in ten minutes, the young man would be killed. He knew, of course, that his choice was the life of his son or the lives of all the people in the Alcazar. The Communist put the boy on the phone, who said, "Father, they tell me they will kill me if you do not surrender the Alcazar." His father replied, "Then, cry out to God, my son, and go to your death bravely." He added, "I love you, my son—good-bye." The boy said, "Good-bye, father—I love you, too." Then, to the Communist leader the father said, "Don't wait the ten minutes you offered; the Alcazar will never be surrendered." It never was, and it became the rallying point for the Loyalist forces. Our hosts gave Ron a book, taken from the shelves in that room, which had been ripped through by a bullet.

Those were marvelous, exciting, and interesting years, and, as it turned out, they would lead to ones that were even more so. As I have said, Ronnie's name was first put in nomination at the Republican Convention in 1968. That was the first time I sat in a convention hall and heard all the hoopla and demonstrations that go with a nomination.

Then came 1975, and we began to get more and more mail, phone calls, personal visits from people asking Ronnie to run for the presidency in 1976. Contrary to what many assume, he wasn't sure he wanted to run and really didn't decide definitely until not long before he announced. Again, I had mixed emotions. I knew he'd make a good president, and I was proud that people would think of my husband for the position, but it's such an awesome responsibility it almost seems too much for one man, especially today. So many things went through my mind—the complete change in our lives, the changes to be faced by the children. Before these thoughts could take hold completely, we were off on the campaign trail.

When he ran for the presidential nomination in 1976, Ronnie didn't have the support of the so-called Republican establishment, the hierarchy, nor did he have it when he ran for governor the first time. What he had, though, was grass-roots support—from the people. This was fine with me, but I couldn't quite understand the party. He's traveled all over the country to help elect Republicans from all points of the party spectrum when asked. And he's been asked many, many times. The first time he ran for governor, he had no record to show what he could do, but after that he had a track record. There seems to be an inconsistency here somewhere. But if our support had to be limited, I'd want it from the people.

A presidential campaign is an experience not to be equalled.

Right after the announcement in Washington, we flew to Miami. We were on a platform, and a man called out "Hi, Dutch—glad to see you." Anytime anyone says "Dutch" we know he's from the Midwest, where Ronnie was once a sports announcer and used that nickname. Ronnie recognized him and said, "Hi, I'll be down to see you afterward."

As a candidate, Ronnie had just been joined by the Secret Service men. They had told him to turn left when he came down from the platform. Instead, he turned right in order to see his old friend. I followed behind him with "Tommy" Thomas, our Florida chairman. We had gone only a few steps when I heard Tommy yell, "What the hell do you think you're doing?" And he turned and plunged into the crowd.

It turned out that he had spotted a young man with a gun. Tommy is a tall, large man, but he was very courageous to act as he did. The Secret Service moved in quickly, but it took a lot of effort to subdue this twenty-year-old, who was very strong.

Ronnie had turned when he heard the commotion and saw a child in trouble behind a rope that had been strung to keep the crowd back. When a crowd like this pushes from the rear, it presses forward on those in front. The little boy was in front and had fallen forward with the rope catching him under the chin. Ronnie turned to help him, but before he could move, the Secret Service men had literally carried him away to safety. I had been shoved into a nearby building for safekeeping.

When they took the gun away from the young man, it turned out to be a toy. But it certainly looked real, and our emotions were certainly real. Later, I said to Ronnie, "I don't care who says 'Dutch' from now on, if the Secret Service says turn left, we turn left." Ronnie laughed and agreed, but it was quite a beginning to a campaign. Isn't it a shame we've come to this in our country, or in the world for that matter?

But, as we campaigned, my regard and respect for the people increased tenfold. I saw this country as I never had before. It's an experience I wish everyone could have just once. The days and nights do become a jumble, though, and one place melts into another. There are so many hotels and motels, so many long days of never being able to wash your face till just before you fall into bed, exhausted, at midnight—after having started at dawn.

When Ronnie and I were on separate schedules, again I held question-and-answer sessions and found, as before, that people's concerns are the same no matter where they live. There is nothing regional about them. They worry about big government and individual freedom, high taxes, inflation, recession, the breakdown in family life and morals, the young and the old.

Mike and Maureen were out campaigning and giving speeches, too, and working hard. Ron was working also, but in the background. He didn't want to be out front, but traveled on the plane with us, hauled luggage, helped with the news releases, and set up microphones for the press corps. Ron learned plenty about how a campaign actually works. He never wanted anyone to know who he was, and, I must say, the press never blew the whistle on him, for which I was grateful.

Now that I've mentioned it, I'd like to say that one of the nice things that came out of the campaign was that the press (really all the news media) got to know us better, and we got to know them better. I thought they treated us fairly and, by the end of the campaign, felt that we had made some new friends and that there was better understanding than there had been before. I've saved some of the thank-you notes they wrote me afterward because they meant a great deal.

Of course, by the time we reached Kansas City for the Republican National Convention, the emotion and tension had risen considerably and everything became something of a blur, but it was exciting. The only thing I regretted was that the Republican National Committee had assigned us a box that was way down at one end of the auditorium, completely separate from the crowd. You don't get to choose your box! To make it worse, there was a glass partition between me and the people. It was frustrating, to say the least. I'll always be grateful to the alternate delegates from Colorado who switched tags with me and the children so that we could go down and sit in their section. It was as close to the California delegation as I could get, but at least I could be with the crowds and really feel the excitement. It was a wonderful experience, and a long way from Bethesda, Maryland, to be sure.

Because the experience is so exciting, you find you have only bits and pieces of things you remember. Of course, I remember being greeted warmly by the delegates when I came into the arena each night. I remember the night Ron called me from the arena at the hotel when I hadn't planned on going and asked me to come over. I dressed as quickly as I could and hurried over. I also remember being told that on the last night all the Reagan signs had been taken away from our box, but that our kids had gone there early and pasted them all back up before we arrived. All those memories—and many more—will stay with me always.

In the days leading up to the convention, the excitement kept mounting. Once the primaries and the various state party conventions were over, the press began to guess daily at the delegates' tallies. Ronnie and Gerald Ford seemed to be almost neck and neck, with quite a few delegates still listed as uncommitted.

At the 1972 convention, the delegates created a committee to devise an improved method of selecting a vice-presidential candidate—improved, that is, over the old last-minute-choice method. Ronnie decided, after consulting with his people in mid-July, to announce his choice of candidate before the August convention.

He asked Senator Richard Schweiker from Pennsylvania to be his running mate. Before all of this happened, they had a nearly daylong meeting together, and Ronnie was convinced that Senator Schweiker would follow his policies and principles. They also like each other (the Schweikers are good friends of ours to this day).

As it turned out, the night prior to the evening of the actual nomination balloting proved to be the climactic one. That was the night the convention's rules were to be adopted, and a major struggle had developed over something called Rule 16-C. This rule would have required each candidate to announce his vice-presidential choice prior to the nomination balloting. Since the committee created by the previous convention had not come in with recommendations for new vice-presidential selection procedures, this proposed rule change was the alternative. The tension mounted throughout the evening. Emotions ran high, as they always do at national political conventions when a climactic moment is at hand. When the vote was taken on Rule 16-C, it went against us by a narrow margin, 1,180 to 1,089. As it turned out, that vote on the rule change was closely reflected in the nomination balloting the next night. Ford—1,187; Reagan—1,070. Though we had not won, the platform was very much a "delegates' platform," not one dictated by party hierarchy, and it also closely reflected Ronnie's views. President Ford came over to the hotel that night, as had been agreed upon before. He and Ronnie met privately and then appeared jointly for the press.

The morning after the nomination, Ronnie held meetings with his delegation and workers to thank them. I didn't go to the first meeting, but I was told that after he thanked them, he quoted from an old Scottish ballad, "I'm hurt but I'm not slain, I'll lie me down and rest a bit and then I'll fight again." I don't think any of the delegates there will ever forget it.

I joined him for the second meeting with all the workers, and when we got up on the platform to face the young people who had come from all over the country on their own to work and campaign in Ronnie's behalf, we realized that, almost without exception, they were crying. Ronnie thanked them for all they had done and told them to not let this loss discourage them.

215

He told them that they had now seen the inner workings of politics, that they should not give up their ideals and principles, should not turn to expediency, and, above all, should not let this make them cynical. "It's the cause that's important and the cause goes on," he concluded. Looking at those youthful, tearful faces, I had to hide my own tears. I knew Ronnie was having difficulty, too, but he managed to say, "There are millions and millions of young people out there who want what you want, who want it to be as we do, who want it to be a shining city on a hill." "A shining city on a hill"—we left the room on those words, and my heart ached for all those young people, whose faces I couldn't bear to look at any longer, and for my husband—such a wonderful, lovable, decent man.

As a candidate, he wasn't supposed to attend the earlier convention proceedings, so that last night he made his first personal appearance. The demonstration it set off was simply astonishing. And it was completely unexpected, especially for Ronnie. We rose from our seats over and over again and waved in response. Finally, they started to yell, "Speech." Ronnie tried to motion that that was impossible. He told Frank Reynolds of ABC that it "was someone else's night." He didn't think he should make a speech—a typical understated Ronnie remark.

Later as the evening went on and President Ford made his acceptance speech, he ended by turning to our box and asking Ronnie to come down to the podium, adding "Bring Nancy with you." As we were on our way, Ronnie turned to me and said, "If he asks me to say anything, I don't know what I can say beyond thank you." We arrived at the podium to join the Fords, the Bob Doles, the Rockefellers, and party officials. I'll never forget that night as long as I live. We looked out at an auditorium where everyone was standing and no one ever sat down. When Ronnie started to speak, you could have heard a pin drop. From somewhere deep within him, the words started to come out. He, who didn't know what he was going to say, spoke so eloquently, so movingly, so poignantly. He started by thanking everyone, and then he paused and said,

If I could just take a moment, I had an assignment the

other day. Someone asked me to write a letter for a time capsule that is going to be opened in Los Angeles a hundred years from now, on our Tricentennial.

It sounded like an easy assignment. They suggested I write about the problems and issues of the day. And I set out to do so, riding down the coast in an automobile, looking at the blue Pacific out on one side and the Santa Ynez Mountains on the other, and I couldn't help but wonder if it was going to be as beautiful a hundred years from now as it was on that summer day.

And then I tried to write—let your own mind turn to that task. You're going to write for people a hundred years from now who know all about us, we know nothing about them. We don't know what kind of a world they'll be living in. Suddenly I thought to myself, If I write of the problems, they'll be the domestic problems of which the President spoke here tonight; the challenges confronting us, the erosion of freedom taking place under Democratic rule in this country, the invasion of private rights, the controls and restrictions on the vitality of the great free economy that we enjoy. These are the challenges that we must meet and then again there is that other challenge of which we spoke that we live in a world in which the great powers have poised and aimed at each other horrible missiles of destruction, nuclear weapons that can in minutes arrive at each other's country and destroy virtually the civilized world we live in.

And suddenly it dawned on me; those who would read this letter a hundred years from now will know whether those missiles were fired. They will know whether we met our challenges. Whether they will have the freedom that we have known up until now will depend on what we do here. Will they look back with appreciation and say, Thank God for those people in 1976 who headed off the loss of freedom? Who kept us now a hundred years later free? Who kept our world from nuclear destruction? And if we fail they probably won't get to read the letter at all because it speaks of individual freedom and they won't be allowed to talk of that or read of it.

This is our challenge and this is why we're here in this hall tonight. Better than we've ever done before, we've got to quit talking to each other and about each other and go out and communicate to the world that we may be fewer in number than we've ever been but we carry the message they've been waiting for. We must go forth from here united, determined that what a great general said a few years ago is true; "There is no substitute for victory."

When he finished, it brought the cheers he deserved. Then, we said our good-byes and took our leave with the sound of the applause and "California, Here I Come" ringing in our ears.

Ronnie and I both felt that we came away from the campaign a good deal richer than before. We had no regrets. We both believe everything happens for a reason, though it may be hard to understand at the time. It's painful to lose, of course. It's terribly disappointing when you've worked so hard. But I was proud of Ronnie. He had conducted himself and his campaign with dignity and integrity. Before we went down to the arena that last night, we had a glass of champagne and I told him in all the years we'd been married he had never done anything to disappoint me. God must have thought a lot of me to have given him to me.

We were touched by our friends who were with us and by the newspeople who came up and said they had enjoyed being with us. Frank Reynolds said, "Maybe I never said it, but I like traveling with you. I'm going to miss you and I wish you well." It meant a lot.

So we came back to California and went to our beloved ranch for a little rest. It wasn't long before Ronnie was taping television spots, raising money, and making speeches for the party and President Ford and the whole Republican ticket. When the 1976 campaign was over, his own travel and speaking schedule took over, and he resumed his radio commentary and newspaper column.

The years have passed. Who knows now where our paths will lead us? Life has a lot to offer, and I've been blessed by the opportunity to be more a part of it than most—certainly more than I had ever dreamed of—and I'm grateful for that.

Over the years there have been some wonderful "tomorrows" that became treasured yesterdays. I don't know now what tomorrow will bring, but like Scarlett, I guess, I'll think about it . . . tomorrow. Meanwhile, there is a lot of living to do today.